MAULED

We would like to also take this opportunity to acknowledge the traditional territories upon which we live and work. In Calgary, Alberta, we acknowledge the Niitsítapi (Blackfoot) and the people of the Treaty 7 region in Southern Alberta, which includes the Siksika, the Piikuni, the Kainai, the Tsuut'ina, and the Stoney Nakoda First Nations, including Chiniki, Bearpaw, and Wesley First Nations. The City of Calgary is also home to Métis Nation of Alberta, Region III. In Victoria, British Columbia, we acknowledge the traditional territories of the Lkwungen (Esquimalt and Songhees), Malahat, Pacheedaht, Scia'new, T'Sou-ke, and W̱SÁNEĆ (Pauquachin, Tsartlip, Tsawout, Tseycum) peoples.

MAULED

*Lessons Learned from
a Grizzly Bear Attack*

Crosbie Cotton
Jeremy Evans

RMB

For information on purchasing bulk quantities of this book, or to
obtain media excerpts or invite the author to speak at an event, please
visit rmbooks.com and select the "Contact" tab.

RMB | Rocky Mountain Books Ltd.
rmbooks.com
@rmbooks
facebook.com/rmbooks

Cataloguing data available from Library and Archives Canada
ISBN 9781771604833 (paperback)
ISBN 9781771604840 (electronic)

Cover and interior design by Colin Parks
Cover photo by heckepics (iStock)

Printed and bound in Canada

We acknowledge the financial support of the Government of Canada
through the Canada Book Fund and the Canada Council for the Arts,
and of the province of British Columbia through the British Columbia
Arts Council and the Book Publishing Tax Credit.

Disclaimer
The views expressed in this book are those of the authors and do
not necessarily reflect those of the publishing company, its staff, or
its affiliates.

CONTENTS

A NOTE FROM THE PUBLISHER

In order to clearly demonstrate the extent of Jeremy's injuries and how remarkable his recovery has been, the authors and publisher have decided to include a photo (eighth page of the insert starting after page 96) after much discussion and consideration. We understand that the graphic nature of the image is disturbing, but we hope that readers will respect this decision and empathize with the author in terms of the long road to recovery that he has endured.

Three Years Before

Enthusiastic, passionate, determined, intensely focused, and bent on success — these are some of the traits for which Jeremy Evans is renowned. On September 5, 2014, Jeremy and his friend Nathan went deer hunting early in the morning to one of their favourite areas, near Strathmore, about 50 kilometres east of Calgary. They set up in a blind at ground level as Jeremy, at the time an independent electrical contractor, participated in a conference call — he had recently landed his biggest cell-phone tower building contract ever.

As Jeremy talked business details, Nathan spotted several deer bedding down in the distance. Once the call ended, the two men came up with a plan. Jeremy would go one way to climb into his tree stand, about eight to ten metres off the ground. Nathan would go fully around the property to approach the herd from behind, steering them towards Jeremy.

As Jeremy climbed into his tree stand, one of the screw-in steps gave way, sending him at least eight metres to the ground, where he landed on both feet with a resounding thud. Although his left ankle initially hurt a bit, Jeremy wrote it off as a minor sprain. He climbed back up to the stand and waited for Nathan to push the deer within range. Jeremy waited in anticipation, his ankle throbbing, but Nathan was unsuccessful — he was not able to move the herd to within bow range before they had to leave.

When the two returned to the truck, Jeremy took two large screwdrivers, inserting them into his boot to hold the ankle in place. He then solidly taped up the whole boot and ankle. After dropping Nathan off, he went to pick up his friend Wayne for an afternoon of hunting.

"Wayne asked what had happened, and I told him," remembers Jeremy. "He asked if I needed to go to the hospital, and I said no, I probably just sprained it. I told him let's get going, I saw a big buck among the does out in Strathmore that we should be able to stalk."

Sure enough, the buck was bedded down with does when the two arrived at the familiar spot in Strathmore. They approached the large buck stealthily and slowly — very, very slowly in Jeremy's case, as he was in excruciating pain from his ankle injury. They followed the buck until finally Wayne came sufficiently close to shoot it. Pulling the buck to the truck in sweltering heat was also a challenging ordeal, as Jeremy had no strength in his left leg. Wayne drove. Jeremy could barely move when they dropped off the animal at the butcher. After taking Wayne home, and at Wayne's insistence, Jeremy headed to the hospital, arriving at about seven p.m., roughly 12 hours after falling from the tree.

When the x-ray technician asked him to remove the boot, Jeremy could not do it. Ultimately, she was able to cut the tape off and remove the screwdrivers, handing them to Jeremy in disbelief. Finally, the boot came off as Jeremy writhed in pain. Says Jeremy: "As soon as my boot came off, my ankle like doubled in size. It was green and black."

The x-rays showed that not only had Jeremy broken the ankle, he had also torn the ligaments that hold the three main bones in place. After a pin was inserted to help the ankle heal, a full boot-style walking cast followed that came up to Jeremy's knee. Jeremy drove himself home. His wife, Joyce, an aquatic biologist, was away for the weekend doing fieldwork.

Unbelievably, such was his passion for the outdoors, Jeremy decided to go hunting again the next day, walking cast, crutches and all. He returned to Strathmore and was able to get a doe. He didn't climb the tree with his cast. Everything occurred at ground level.

There was still the cellphone tower to build in Edmonton, a project almost ten times the dollar value of any Jeremy had previously bid for and landed. He would not let the broken ankle thwart success. Although he would use subcontractors for some specific tasks, Jeremy, functioning as general contractor, would handle most of the work himself.

"I cut the pavement, dug the hole, installed the ground grid and the rebar myself," says Jeremy. "I did this on a broken ankle in seven business days. It was the biggest job of my career. I took a huge risk taking on the job and pulled it off."

That was his forte — taking risks and pulling them off. Until the day an enraged grizzly bear attacked.

CHAPTER I

Five Days Before the Mauling

DON LOGAN FIRST MET JEREMY EVANS THE SUNDAY before the devastating grizzly bear mauling, and six days before the hunting season opened for bighorn sheep. It was an energized day of outdoor learning the ultra-marathoner will never forget.

Both Don and Jeremy were married to aquatic biologists, and it was their wives who encouraged them to meet for a day of mountain biking and fly-fishing. They thought their husbands were a good match to become friends. Jeremy's wife, Joyce, also worried about his frequent journeys alone deep into the wild, far from any other human presence. Don's wife, Andria, was aware her husband wanted to learn more about the new province they now called home.

A specialist in emergency management, Don had moved from Nova Scotia to join the National Energy Board (now the Canada Energy Regulator) as an environmental inspection and resource conservation officer. He yearned to become more knowledgeable about the famed Canadian Rocky Mountains and the wildlife that made those jagged peaks home. A novice hunter, he wanted to experience all that Alberta had to offer and hoped Jeremy would be his ticket to greater understanding.

"That day, Jeremy was absolutely incredible, with unlimited energy and so much knowledge," recalls Don. "Inside his head he carries a visual map of where all animals are around him and what they are all doing. I had never seen anyone like him. He has an extremely keen feel for the surrounding environment. He can spot animals that are only tiny specks in the distance."

The two met that morning near the multi-cabin Lodge at Panther River, which bills itself as a wilderness resort with a dash of luxury. Its motto: "Escape into the Wild." It is located almost 60 kilometres along mostly gravel roads from the nearest sizable town, Sundre (population about 2,700). Home to renowned backcountry outfitters Panther River, the surrounding Burnt Timber and Panther drainages have abundant whitetail deer, mule deer, elk, moose, bighorn sheep, black bears, grizzly bears, wolves and cougars.

From there, Don and Jeremy headed almost 16 kilometres along the dangerous, twisting Panther Road, which sports large warning signs: travel at your own risk; vehicle traffic not recommended. The road had been built to access gas and oil drilling sites in the remote area. It is also dotted with signs setting the maximum speed at 15 kilometres per hour and cautioning that steep grades are ahead. They parked just off a rutted gravel road, where a metal gate barred off-road vehicle access to a trail leading to a decades-old family-owned outfitters' camp. The short trip had taken almost 45 minutes.

The Panther River Valley and the Burnt Timber drainage were — and remain — two of Jeremy's favourite places. To proclaim them far from the madding crowd would be the understatement of the century. Jeremy and Joyce had discovered them years earlier, when the two avid anglers were looking for a suitable place to camp for the weekend. They found a perfect, panoramic spot atop the headwaters of North Burnt Timber Creek, but their first camping trip ended suddenly when they came face to face with two enormous, growling grizzly bears.

Straight ahead, for as far the eye could see, was Banff National Park and the mind-numbing beauty of the Canadian Rockies. To the left was Kananaskis Country and the awesome Peter Lougheed Provincial Park. To the right was the Ya Ha Tinda Valley, once home to large numbers of prehistoric bison. Today more than 1,000 elk winter at the Ya Ha Tinda Ranch, where Parks Canada raises its horses for warden use across Canada.

Don and Jeremy had planned to bike maybe 40 kilometres and do some fly-fishing. Jeremy also wanted to reach a mountain plateau to see if he could spot the specks of any bighorn sheep nestled high in the mountaintops several kilometres away. At six foot two and 236 pounds, Jeremy was in terrific shape. The sheep season would open the upcoming Friday.

Jeremy was also excited to try out his newest treasure — a Specialized Rockhopper. The $1,500 hardtail all-mountain bike was much lighter and more versatile than the heavy downhill bike he had been using to blast off jumps and soar over other structures during extreme rides down ski resort slopes. As a first-time father with a new daughter, Jeremy had decided to abandon the crazy extreme sports he had enjoyed for many years. And the new bike was much easier to pedal up mountainsides.

As an endurance runner himself, Don was no physical slouch. Yet he had trouble keeping up as the two climbed on their bikes to pedal the rutted, rugged rudimentary horse trail about 14 kilometres up towards the treed ridge. They crossed the creek many times. In several places it had braided into five to ten smaller channels during the 100-year flood of 2013. Although the water was easily forded, it was a gruelling climb. Once they arrived at the sheep-hunt scouting site, about 50 metres above the river, the landscape was epic, as Don would later describe it, with nothing to spoil the viewscape — just a spectacular panorama of trees, mountains and rivers that seemed to go on forever.

After the scouting, it was time for fly-fishing. On their bikes they headed downriver about a kilometre to begin casting for bull trout, a long, slim fish named for its larger head and mainly found in pools instead of fast-running water. Although Don had fished in Nova Scotia, what he learned that day was eye-popping. Jeremy — a stern but patient teacher, totally engaged in the task at hand — taught Don how to crouch and hide under branches so the fish would not see him. Don learned which hand to cast with, as he usually did it the wrong way. He learned better ways to cast the fly. "It was incredible for me. Jeremy just knows so much and is amazingly focused. He even makes his own fishing equipment." After catching a few, they released them — bull trout are a threatened species in Alberta and cannot be eaten.

As they walked their bikes downriver, Don heard a jaw cracking and something big moving up above, in the trees. He could smell an animal and kept hearing a popping sound. Almost nonchalantly, Jeremy just kept moving along the embankment until he reached a pool where a massive multi-pound bull trout was swimming. It was the largest either Jeremy or Don had ever seen.

Hiding behind branches, they tried many times to catch the giant fish by casting flies, including several that simply bounced off its back. Jeremy had enough. He jumped in the pool and just picked the fish up. They took pictures holding it. Then it was Don's turn to jump in after the fish. As his knees smashed against the rocks, he was glad he had worn his bike knee pads that day.

Seeing no path back up to the ridge and ultimately on to the trail to where his vehicle was parked, Jeremy decided the only way to go was straight up the steep embankment. They bushwhacked up the mountainside, taking small steps while advancing their bikes. "It was slow and grinding. It took hours," recalls Don. "I kept thinking, *When is he ever going to stop? Where is he getting all that energy?* After what seemed an eternity, they finally reached the top, where Jeremy once again paused to scout for sheep up the valley.

The ride down was a hair-raising one for Don, even though he was a veteran rider. Never had he gone so fast on a mountain bike. He learned a new technique — leap-frogging, where one rider races ahead down the mountain and then waits for the other, to ensure he is safe. Then the order is reversed. Don estimates they hit speeds up to 50 kilometres per hour on the rugged and often nasty horse trail. They crossed the creek several times, but it took only a brief time to travel the more than 14 kilometres.

The two were planning to meet again the day before the opening of bighorn sheep season. They would hunt and camp together for the weekend. Don was extremely confident he would once again enjoy intense hands-on learning from an expert outdoorsman in a spectacular environment. His spine tingled at the thought of what might lie ahead. But when the day arrived, Don was not able to join Jeremy. So — reluctantly, and to Joyce's dismay — Jeremy went alone.

Bighorn sheep hunting is one of the most physically and mentally demanding hunting experiences available in the mountains. Sometimes called the "monarchs of the crags," bighorns inhabit exceedingly rugged terrain. They are usually found nestled in rocks two-thirds of the way up a mountain, intently watching the ground below to spot, and then flee from, predators. After spotting one in the distance, a hunter can then take hours climbing several thousand vertical feet to approach it from above, evading its keen sense of smell. As Jeremy says: "All the time, you are either going up a cliff or down a cliff."

As was his normal procedure, Jeremy headed out Thursday, the day before the season opened. He was keen to get the camp set up and do some advance scouting of where the bighorn might be hiding. He knew the best time to spot rams is at daybreak, when they move from their bedding area to feed nearby.

That evening, Don was stunned when he heard the news broadcast. Earlier that day, a hunter had been viciously mauled by a bear west of Sundre. Andria texted Joyce, asking whether that hunter was Jeremy. It was.

CHAPTER 2

Jeremy and Joyce: A Love Story

JEREMY WAS PLAYING CHESS WITH A FRIEND AT JAMES Fowler High School in Calgary when Joyce walked by. He thought she was cute and was enthralled that she was considered a nerd with a love of biology and the sciences. A Grade 12 graduating student, Jeremy told his friend he was going to take her as his date to the prom. His friend replied bluntly: "Forget it, she is out of your league."

But as with everything else in Jeremy's life, when he sets a goal to achieve something, he lets little, if anything, stand in his way. His courtship of Joyce was conducted in a responsible, considerate and gentlemanly manner — he treats others the way he likes to be treated.

Joyce was nervous at first. She was only in Grade 10, at an age where two years' difference seemed enormous. At six foot two and 130 pounds, with a lean build, Jeremy was known for his long-distance running records and played defensive back on the school's football team. They rode the same bus to school and back, and Jeremy, pretending to live close to her home, started getting off at her stop so they could talk while he walked her home. Once she was inside, he would walk to his own home, almost 1.6 kilometres away.

Joyce was his date at the prom that year. He was her first-ever boyfriend. Jeremy had only had one girlfriend in his life, and he broke up with her the day he met Joyce.

The two shared much in common, including a love of the outdoors and especially fly-fishing. Although not much of a hunter, Joyce enjoyed hiking, cross-country skiing and birdwatching, having grown up in a family that valued camping and spending time in nature. It is exceptionally fitting that her career choice was to become an aquatic biologist. She was also highly creative, particularly in the visual arts.

It was together, on an August long weekend when Jeremy was about 19 years old, that they found the Panther River, the adjacent Burnt Timber drainage area and the spot Jeremy would later use as a base camp for his hunting trips. It was their first time in the area; they were looking for a new place to camp and to fish. Sporting backpacks, they were walking the trail when the Turner family came alongside in a horse and wagon, bringing supplies to their Burnt Timber outfitter camp, which they called home during the summers. The Turners and their children are legendary in the region: outfitters, dairy farmers, community volunteers, outdoorsmen and -women, great hunters, ranchers, rodeo superstars; they epitomized country life.

The dad, Bobby Turner, offered Joyce a ride but refused to let Jeremy onto the wagon, or even let him load his backpack into it. For the chivalrous Turners, women ride; men walk. Joyce declined the ride; however, she was grateful for the Turners' carrying her camping bag on the wagon for several kilometres. Over the years, Bobby would frequently chastise Jeremy for going alone on his mountain bike so deep into the wilderness. He knew danger is always present in the forest.

Bobby was the patriarch of the family, a larger-than-life character with a penchant for making people laugh. The son of a bird and big-game hunter who purchased a family ranch near Calgary in 1925, Bobby started professional outfitting in 1968, taking bighorn sheep hunters into the Rocky Mountains. Enthusiastic about preserving the uniqueness of the area, he volunteered on the Panther River Advisory Committee and Panther River Environmental Enhancement Legacy Committee, which led to an environmental studies university scholarship being named after him.

The family company, Alberta Bighorns Ltd., has guided hunters from around the world and is the only outfitter in that area with bighorn sheep tags for hunters outside Alberta and outside Canada. Bobby's wife, Sunni, a former schoolteacher famous for her trademark bright red cowboy hat, is a successful hunter in her own right — she once harvested the largest Dall sheep of the hunting season in the Northwest Territories. All five of their sons have guided for the family company, and sons Norman and Jim Turner took over in 2013. Bobby passed away in 2016.

Joyce and Jeremy's search for the perfect camping spot started anew soon after they reached the outfitters' tent. The rustic camp had been developed with care in the middle of deep wilderness; clients quoted on their website rave about the "top notch," "unbelievable" facilities.

Jeremy and Joyce found a spot on a scenic ridge in the North Burnt Timber drainage guarded with some trees and offering a splendid panorama of the area. It was a place they would always consider special; few people ever go that far into the backcountry. That afternoon, they explored the North Burnt Timber Creek; the next day, they headed out to fish. Barely 300 metres from camp, walking through the thick willows along a trail, Jeremy stopped suddenly. He was about five metres in front of Joyce. He crouched down, looked back at Joyce, and said quietly, with authority, "Get down."

Two huge grizzlies, one to the right of the trail and the other to the left, stood on their hind legs, loudly snapping their jaws. They seemed startled, looking for the culprits who had interrupted their quest. It was only five seconds before both bears bolted down into the drainage, but for Jeremy and Joyce it felt like forever. After realizing the danger that lurked down in the valley, they headed quickly back to camp, planning to move higher up the valley or head to another valley. As they packed up, the tension in the air was almost overwhelming. Jeremy kept looking down the trail to see if the grizzlies were coming back. Both he and Joyce were extremely nervous. Partway though taking down the tent, Joyce noticed movement down the trail.

That was enough. They were not sure if it was the bears or just the wind blowing leaves around, but they tossed on their packs, grabbed the rest of the camping gear and hightailed it out of there, carrying most of the equipment in their arms and hands. They headed to the outfitter camp, where they knew it was safe. Bobby and Sunni were there with two of their sons; they invited Jeremy and Joyce to stay for dinner. They talked about their passion for the outdoors while chowing down on some of the best chili Jeremy and Joyce had ever had. It was the beginning of an enduring friendship that lasts to this day.

Jeremy and Joyce were married in August 2011, at Boundary Ranch, in Kananaskis Country, a spectacular location in the Rocky Mountains, perfectly fitting for two people who thrive on the outdoors. For their honeymoon they went — you guessed it — fishing, on Vancouver Island. Joyce recalls they caught tons of salmon. Jeremy quickly determined he was not a boat person. He got seasick.

CHAPTER 3

The Attack, in Jeremy's Words

AS WAS TRADITIONAL WHEN HUNTING IN THE BURNT Timber drainage, I left my Calgary home in total darkness just after midnight on Thursday, August 24, for the three-hour drive to where I always parked my Ford 150. Less than three weeks earlier, I had turned 32 years old. I had a 100-pound pack for the planned three-day camping trip, which for me would be considered a light backpack. My goal that day was to set up camp and pre-scout for bighorn sheep in anticipation of opening day.

Spotting them is the tough part, especially off in the distance. Their grey fur blends in perfectly with the rock and shale. I knew my best chance was to use the rising sun, and to look for moving shadows on the open grassy slopes where they like to feed. I planned on opening day to get way into the back bowl, like I did every year, hoping that other hunters would push them to the bowl, where I would be waiting. Sheep hunters know the first day can be extremely frustrating, and entertaining. There is always a guy walking the ridge not knowing what he is doing, which this time, I hoped, could work in my favour, as sheep flee to safety. The escape bowl was reserved for "crazy people," as Bobby Turner liked to describe me. I was certain this was my year to finally fold a tag on a ram. I had spent several years watching the rams and figuring out what they do. I had a jump-start and was absolutely excited for this season.

It was around three a.m. when I finally made it to the old dirt trail that led me back to some of the most magnificent countryside I have ever gotten the chance to experience. I parked my truck on the same set of ruts I had used so many times before, often to go fly-fishing with my wife. It was where Don Logan and I had parked the other day. I was known to other locals that hunt the area as the "Crazy One" on the mountain bike who goes way back in, where the trails fade in the landscape. I loved going back in there because I never saw anyone. I remember Bobby telling me about the kinds of sheep hunters that he sees every year. There were the day hunters and ridge walkers that only go three to five kilometres in; the outfitters, who start just out of reach of the day hunters; and there was me, the "Crazy One," who just headed straight for the most untouched of places.

There are no driveable roads into the area, which is mostly why I love it so much. The chance of being in the greatest of the great outdoors, enjoying the peace and quiet with no one around, would without doubt be any outdoor enthusiast's dream. I knew I was simply so lucky to be able to enjoy the magnificent scenery that morning. With my truck parked, the adrenalin kicked in.

I got suited up and then strapped on my trusty Badlands pack that has carried my gear on many adventures into the wilderness. I had been testing hunting products for the Badlands company for years. With everything loaded up in my pack, I hopped on my bike in my hunting gear and started down the long, winding 14-kilometre trail that would lead me to my spike camp at the headwaters of the North Burnt Timber Creek. It would be my camping home for the next three days. With only a small sliver of the moon and the stars lighting the way, I sped towards the Turner outfitter camp in anticipation of Bobby sitting next to his makeshift table, drinking his coffee in the moonlight, waiting for sunrise to get a jump-start at spotting some sheep. I knew he would be chastising me again for going alone deep into the back-country. To my surprise, Bobby was not there, and the camp seemed empty. I started to get more excited, as now there was less competition. Further along the way, I came across another camp, where two cowboys were sitting around a campfire cooking breakfast in the moonlight. My excitement faded a little bit as I rode my bike past their camp along the trail.

Shortly after nine a.m., I finally made it to where the trails fade into the landscape. This was the point where

I had to carry my bike across a minefield of boulders as I climbed up the very narrow steep side of a drainage to enter the edge of the treeline. It was so gruellingly steep I had to walk my bike up the slope. Located about 12 kilometres from where I started, the top featured a small, relatively flat plateau and a thick willow undergrowth that filled the gaps between the staggered spruce. It was perfect to sneak through while looking for sheep in between the trees. As I peered through the trees in various places, stopping about every three or four metres, I frequently rested my hands on the handlebars to hold my arms steady from the excitement of what I might find. It also helped to maintain my balance on the steep hillside. I was almost at my spot, where I normally sit and eat my traditional breakfast of oatmeal and hot apple cider. I approached it, sipping on the cider, looking again for sheep. I could see into two back bowls. Filled with excitement, I got a glimpse of a shiny grey brow shimmering off in the distance on the edge of one bowl, where sheep usually are found. I got pretty excited, took my pack off and rested it against my bike and pulled on my binoculars to get a better look. Sure enough, it was ewes and lambs — but still always exciting to see sheep!

I watched them intently for longer than I should have, as this was early in the season, when rams are not usually found with the ewes. Nonetheless, you try to imagine them years later with the full curl horns hunters like me dream of. As I brought down my binoculars to end that imaginary sheep dream, I heard a noise and caught a flash of brown just out of the corner of my eye. It appeared right in front of me, maybe three or four metres away. It only took me a fraction of a second to realize what it was — a bear cub. I started to reach down to my pack to grab my bear spray. I knew I was in trouble. It was an "Oh, Shit!" moment.

As an expert outdoorsman I could not believe I had packed my bear spray at the bottom of my pack. My gun was also still encased, strapped tightly to my pack. Might as well call me a "granola muncher." When I saw the little brown spot, a sinking feeling enveloped me. It was as if you can see a horrific car accident coming at you and you cannot stop it. I can honestly say it's the first time I have ever felt that way.

I knew mommy was not too far away. As I was cautiously leaning over to open my pack, to arm myself with bear spray, I heard the bush coming alive behind me. The sound of a branch breaking sounded as harsh as a massive crack of thunder. I looked over my right shoulder and there she was, moving at lightning speed less than two metres way. She was on a full run. I could see her mouth open and the glaring whites of her eyes. Everything seemed to be happening in slow motion. Time seemed to almost stop as I anticipated the oncoming pain. It was at that moment I knew I was truly in serious danger.

I had been charged before and sprayed a grizzly once. This was different. This bear had that glossy look in her eyes, with a white sliver glistening on the back edge of her eye. I knew that look. She was not stopping. As I raised my bike up to use as a shield, she was already only centimetres away. Her left paw was stretched out, reaching for me, and her mouth was wide open. I swung my bike in front of her, catching her paw in the rear wheel spokes with her head through the frame of the bike. She was stuck in the bike, but still coming. I quickly grabbed the frame of my pack and started to use it as a shield to block the incoming teeth. I felt like I was in *The Matrix*, dodging bullets in slow motion. There was no time to play dead. This bear was enraged.

I slammed my pack into her head as hard as I could, but she was so strong. I remember seeing her clamp down on my hand, teeth sinking in and the scratching sound of them rubbing on the frame of the pack as she shook her head. I could not feel any pain, but I could see her teeth clearly all the way through my hand. Her strength was unreal. At one point she grabbed my pack and shook it so hard, all I could do was just hold on. When she let go, I made my advance and started to smash her on the head, but she was not backing down.

Then a shimmer of hope emerged after I cracked her a good one on the skull with my pack. She started to back away. I started to make my retreat, backing away slowly but keeping a close eye on her, while trying to get my gun off the pack. I started to feel a sense of relief. But that quickly changed. When about ten metres away, suddenly she turned around and came full tilt towards me. My only thought was to run. I tossed my pack at her, turned and ran up the steep mountainside, hoping to find a tree big enough for me to climb. She closed the gap quickly and was metres away. I jumped from the steep hillside towards her into a tree. She was so close; I could feel the force of her breath against my legs.

I scrambled up the tree, peering down at her and watching her stand up. Showing her impressive size, at least 350 pounds and six feet tall while on her hind legs, she reached up with one of her paws, almost wrapping my right leg with it. Then her head lunged upwards with jaws open. I could see her teeth, and I was thinking to myself, this is going to hurt, as she clamped down on the back side of my right knee. I could feel her teeth sink in, but no pain.

She plucked me right out of that tree like nothing, as grizzlies have about ten times the strength of a powerful human. When I hit the ground, I was dazed but tried to huddle in the underbrush under the tree. I wrapped my arms and legs around the tree. I hung on for dear life, trying to play dead. I could feel her biting my abdomen as she dragged me out from under the tree and tossed me about two metres through the air. She was on top of me instantly.

This would be the start of round two. She grabbed at my skull and bit my face. The first massive bite was on the left side of my face, where her teeth caught me on either side of my eye, crushing the eye socket when she clamped down. I could hear the loud crunch as my bones were crushed into pieces. I could feel my eye in her mouth as it dangled. She was mauling me with intent to kill. Her rancid, disgusting smell hit me as she stood over me, slobbering snot and getting ready for the next bite. It was musty, powerful, like a wet, dripping dog smells coming out of a swamp.

Playing dead was not going to save me from this mad mama. I realized the only chance for survival was to fight back with all my strength. *Fuck this playing dead*, I thought to myself. *It is really hard to play dead when a bear is eating your face.*

Fighting back felt like my only choice. I jammed my thumb up her nose. I poked her in the eyeball. I grabbed her ear as harshly as possible. She was on the right side of my body with her mouth wide open ready to pounce again. I felt her claws raking me.

She readied for another bite. With all the power I could muster, I jammed my arm into her mouth. I remember my fingers sliding down her scarred tongue. It felt like leather as I harshly grabbed onto it and tugged as hard as I could. I pushed with my thumbs under the tongue. I was even capable of getting my forearm down her throat, and she started to vomit. She could not close her mouth. Simultaneously, I reached between her legs and painfully squeezed her crotch as hard as I could. She started to squeal loudly like a screaming pig. Fighting back worked. I let go, and she backed off and ran into the woods.

Once she was out of sight, I stood up, dusted myself off, not yet fully aware of the injuries that I had just endured. I was fully pumped with adrenaline.

I made my way down the slope, through the under-growth back to the trail to my pack with my gun still encased and untouched. I remember saying to myself sarcastically, *Well, that was fun.* I was still hoping to go sheep hunting and enjoy the wilderness for the next several days. I started to remove my firearm from its case. It was covered in slobber and blood. Was it mine? Or the bear's? I struggled to remove my gun from its case. I wondered what was wrong with my fingers. While looking at my hands, trying to make a fist, I could see right through my left hand. The was a hole right through the palm of my hand, in between my ring finger and pinky. My right hand was not looking much better, with a marble-sized hole between my middle and ring finger. What just happened? It still did not make sense to me why I could not move some of my fingers. I was still in a bit of shock, furious over what had just happened and still unaware of the full extent of the injuries I had just endured.

I couldn't help thinking to myself, *that fucking bear,* when the third horrific attack came. It was the worst of them all. I was leaning against a rotten log, knees bent, trying to load my rifle clip. I had the gun leaning against my left shoulder, with the clip in my right hand. I was trying to push in rounds with my thumb. Before I could get the third one in, I heard the sound of ice breaking, followed by the slow motion of my body going limp. I had no control, my arms just dropped to the side. It seemed like an out-of-body experience. I watched my gun fall to the ground as I was pulled away in the brush.

I was being savagely dragged. I could feel the sound of the teeth grinding against the back of my skull. She pulled me in a jerking motion, stopping then pulling me a few feet more each time. This tug-of-war felt like an eternity, but she only pulled me ten or so metres. Once stopped, I was sitting up, propped against her front legs. With one swoop of her right paw, her claws caught me above the right eyebrow, tearing into my scalp and peeling off the right side of my face. I could feel her jaw clicking, teeth grinding on my skull like a dog chewing a bone. I was thinking this was the end, I had no fight left in me. Hell, I could not even move my arms.

She paused, shifting her legs. I fell backwards to the ground. Now she was standing over me on all four legs, straddling my lifeless body, sniffing the air, with her lips curled. It seemed like her victory dance. It was only for a few seconds but felt like minutes. Fierce determination set in. I was not willing to give up and let her finish me off without one last fight. Her hind end now was in line with my shoulders. I reached up with both hands and grabbed what I thought at the time were balls, and squeezed as hard as I could, twisting harshly at the same time. Pulling my back off the ground, hanging on for dear life, I then wrapped my legs around her neck, locking them like a professional MMA fighter. She was bucking like a bronco. I could feel my back scrape across the rocky ground as she twisted and turned running through the brush. She was in excruciating pain; I could feel the terror and shock in her vocal cries that almost sounded again like a squealing pig. I finally had the upper hand. I reluctantly let go. I could hear her crashing through the bush, and her cries fading away.

Dazed, I was in disbelief to still be alive. But where was I? Which way was the trail? At this point I could barely see. I was lying on my back. I reached up, trying to uncover my face. I initially thought I was missing my right eye and more than half of my nose. My left eye was just hanging there with a large section of my hair and eyebrow, drooping down the side of my face. In complete shock, I flipped over to my stomach and tried to stand up, only to slam what was left of my face into the ground. I tried to get a bearing of where I was relative to my pack. All I could see were dark blurry objects that swayed in the breeze. I knew I had to head downhill. The trail was perched along a cliff just above the creek. I started to crawl and felt my way around the thick willows. I got to a slight opening in the brush, which to my surprise was the trail. I decided to crawl up the trail, not knowing if it was the right direction or not. Feeling with my hands, I proceeded up the trail until I felt something remarkably familiar — the smooth wood stock of my rifle. I grabbed it and started feeling around the area frantically for my clip, with no luck.

I used the butt of the gun to help me roll over to my side, then to a sitting position. I remembered I had put a few shells in my pocket. I flipped the bolt of my gun back all the way and tried to put a round in. It kept falling out. I was unable to drop the cartridge directly into the tube. I could not see what I was doing. On all fours, crawling around searching for my clip, I started to panic. Feeling around the ground, I felt something that seemed like a hide. It turned out to be part of my face. I then found an ear. I found several more chunks of flesh and started to pile them up in my right hand. While picking up the last flesh-piece of my face, I finally found my clip!

Loading my gun was still extremely difficult. It was a fight to line up the clip with the stock of the gun. Once the clip was in place, I slammed the bolt forward, and then started firing indiscriminately, hoping to scare off the bear. Since I could not see, I fired a round at anything dark in shape. I may have fired 40 times. I also was hoping someone might hear the shots, come to investigate and help me. The horseback hunters did hear, they later told investigators, but thought it was someone firing a pistol and having fun. They did not come to investigate. The loss of my glasses during the attack made it even more difficult to see. Firing bullets at anything that looked black, I hoped, at minimum might scare the bear away.

I began putting the pieces of my face on the top of my head, bloody skin against bleeding skin to keep the tissue alive. I do not know exactly why. It was not something

I had been taught during extensive first aid and survival training. It was just something I had heard about in high school. One of those pieces was an ear. Another part my scalp. My skull was exposed. My jaw was dangling. My eye was out of its socket. Those steps I took allowed some of my face to be later salvaged and restored.

I used a long-sleeved sweater, put it on upside down with the neck part around my forehead and wrapped the body of the garment around the top and back side of my head. I wrapped the sleeves around to the back of my head, tied a knot and then wrapped the rest of the sleeve under my chin, thus securing it in place. This helped to stem the flow of blood.

Running out of energy, I knew I had to eat something if I was going to have enough energy to keep going. I found some Swedish berries, my favourite candy, and tried to eat them, but they kept falling out of the missing parts of my mouth and jaw. There was no jaw. Trying to eat them was a lost cause. Trying to drink water was an equal failure. I was freaked out.

I could not move. Too many parts of my face were missing, and my body, especially my leg and abdomen, too severely injured. Additionally, I could not see and was deep in a forest far from anyone. I asked myself: *Why continue suffering?*

I placed the barrel of my rifle under my chin and pulled the trigger. It made a clicking sound but did not go off. I moved it to the side and played with the bolt before pulling the trigger again. It went off with a loud bang. The sound scared the hell out of me. I immediately realized putting the gun under my chin was a really stupid thing to do.

Realizing I might not make it out, I scattered the contents of my pack, included orange Hawaiian boxer shorts, to mark my location and to make it easier for someone to find me. I was worried the bear would eat me if I passed out or died on the mountainside. Now, that was certainly a weird thought, but it was a very weird and dangerous situation.

In my pack I was looking for the bright orange emergency blanket I carried. I hoped it would be much easier to spot from the air if rescuers came searching for me. I laid it out, I thought, after I had found the blanket. Fish and Wildlife officers would instead later discover a pair of bright orange underwear laid out neatly on top of the pack. But no emergency blanket.

I also took out the large emergency family-style first aid kit I carried in the pack. I ripped through it, looking for anything I could use to deal with the massive injuries. There was nothing of use at all. Yet I tried to remain as calm as possible. That is what I had learned during survival training at 17 or 18 years old.

My phone was, of course, not getting any signal so deep in the backcountry, but I tried to text my wife anyway. She never received the texts. If I died, I wanted her to know what had happened to me and how much I loved her. The last text she had read from me was one I sent at 2:17 that morning when I was on my way out here. It read: "I love you honey! Take care of the little monster!"

The next dozen or so texts, all undelivered, started flowing at 10:05 a.m., immediately after the mauling. They were filled with spelling errors:

I love you guys so much!

Really ducked up.

Please take care of Abby! Tell her I love her so much! I really wish I could be there! I am so sorry!

I really going to miss you guys!

Please honey please know that I love you so much.

I am dying now all alone.

Whoever finds this please let my wife know I tried to make it.

I am pretty sure this is the end. I am very tired, and I feel like I am going to pass out. If I do I won't wake up. I love you, Honey!! Take good care of the Monster.

I am going to try to make it to the truck. Probably won't make it and will die along the way.

Wish I could be with you one more day and go fish.

I took a selfie of my now missing face. The picture resembled something out of a horror movie. Out of focus because I could not see, it was primarily for Joyce. I wanted her to be able to see what I had endured and how I had tried to make it out of the forest for her and Abby.

Trying to walk, my injured leg simply would not work. I had no balance at all. I must have fallen 100 times in the first 50 metres. Not far from the scene of the attack was the first drainage, where I fell sharply down the steep embankment, tumbling head over heels. I ended up crashing into the rocks far below at the bottom. It was the same trail I had earlier had to walk my bike up because it was too steep to ride up. Lying on the boulders with my arm caught jammed between two of them, I put on some music I had on my phone and tried to gather my thoughts. I had to accept that my life might end this way and stop panicking. As I lay there in the middle of nowhere, I thought:

1. *I can stay here and fall asleep to die.*
2. *I can shoot myself.*
3. *I can make it to the trail and get help.*

Then, unbelievably, the song that started to play on my phone was the absolute favourite of my beautiful red-haired little girl, Abby — "Baby Shark." Our only child at the time, Abby had been born earlier that year. I thought of her. I thought of Joyce. The song stuck on repeat, so it played over and over:

> Baby shark, doo, doo, doo, doo, doo, doo
> Baby shark, doo, doo, doo, doo, doo, doo

Baby shark, doo, doo, doo, doo, doo, doo
Baby shark
Mommy shark, doo, doo, doo, doo, doo, doo
Mommy shark, doo, doo, doo, doo, doo, doo
Mommy shark, doo, doo, doo, doo, doo, doo
Mommy shark
Daddy shark, doo, doo, doo, doo, doo, doo
Daddy shark, doo, doo, doo, doo, doo, doo
Daddy shark, doo, doo, doo, doo, doo, doo
Daddy shark
Grandma shark, doo, doo, doo, doo, doo, doo
Grandma shark, doo, doo, doo, doo, doo, doo
Grandma shark, doo, doo, doo, doo, doo, doo
Grandma shark
Grandpa shark, doo, doo, doo, doo, doo, doo
Grandpa shark, doo, doo, doo, doo, doo, doo
Grandpa shark, doo, doo, doo, doo, doo, doo
Grandpa shark
Let's go hunt, doo, doo, doo, doo, doo, doo
Let's go hunt, doo, doo, doo, doo, doo, doo.

I decided to try to make it to the nearby horse trail, where the chance of someone finding me was much greater. I started crawling up the other side of the steep embankment to get to the horse trail somewhere up above. I had never been forced to climb the opposite side of the drainage, so I had no idea where the main trail actually was located. There was no trail up, so I created one through the bush. I climbed in a straight line, manoeuvring over dead trees, rocks and shrubs, hoping to find the main trail I had biked in on. It took a while, but finally I reached the top. Once I got moving, the pain was less. Guess my brain sort of blocked it out.

CHAPTER 4

The Trip Out

JEREMY WAS ALMOST 14 KILOMETRES FROM HIS truck, in some of the densest forests and most challenging mountain terrain imaginable. Between him and his truck lay two steep drainage basins, 11 creek crossings, the Turner family outfitters' camp and the dreaded last ridge climb, only one kilometre from the trailhead.

His injuries were devastating. He had a complex wound to the face, including his eye socket, jawbone and cheek. The bones were shattered into at least eight pieces. His left eye was hanging down. His nose had been split in half vertically, with the left side hanging by a thin strip of skin. He had a large scalp wound, with his skull exposed. He had a major wound to his hand where the bear had bitten it through his pack. His pinky was fractured. There was a complex wound to his right calf, with tendons severely damaged. His abdominal wall had been damaged during the mauling. And he was bleeding profusely from his face.

After painfully freeing his right arm from the exercise-ball-sized boulders, he had no idea where to find the trail. Still dazed from the tumble, he was unsure of the exact direction he needed to go. After he had tumbled down the embankment, the spot where he had landed was nice, he recalls — relaxing, with the gurgling of a small waterfall nearby. But his goal of survival took precedence over enjoying a peaceful snooze. He decided the safest, quickest way was to go in a straight line. There would be no zigzagging at all because that would expend additional energy, and if he was going to survive, he believed, there would be none extra to spare. Before trying to leave the mauling site, he had covered his arms and shoulders with a sweater. These steps were taken to shield his body from the harsh, pounding sun, which he knew would consume even more of his limited energy.

Up the steep side of the drainage he went. There was no trail to climb. He fell every time he tried to walk, so all he could do was crawl. His right leg, which had been mauled near the knee, could not support any weight. He could barely see at all. Yet Jeremy bushwhacked his way almost 300 metres through dense willows and pockets of dense aspen on a hillside a little too steep for even a horse to climb. At the top of the drainage, he picked the summit of a mountain he recognized in the distance as his focal point, knowing the trail out would cross his path at some point. He made his way towards the next drainage. This one was a lot steeper, almost impassable on horse. After tumbling partway down, he finally found a familiar site, the overgrown old horse trail which he had used to bike in a couple of hours earlier. The initial two kilometres were along the rough horse trail that had been cut into the steep mountainside. In parts it was so steep he had to slide down on his butt. The hill climbs were the worst. All he could do was crawl, although at times he used his gun as a crutch. It was tough, rough and very painful. About two kilometres in, the horse trail merged into a larger main trail.

Jeremy had achieved his first goal. After making it to the main trail, feeling ambitious, he set another goal. Making to the next junction offered a better opportunity to encounter hunters in the area. Along the way he passed a place that was familiar to him, a flat spot just off the main trail where a creek cut the mountainside. This was where Jeremy had set up camp in years past. It had a safe feeling to it. Approaching the creek embankments, he tumbled, doing a harsh face plant into the water. He had reached about the one-third point between the attack site and the outfitters' camp. He knew this measuring point well, and it told him exactly how much progress he had made. He drank fresh water to hydrate, filled with excitement that everything afterwards was mainly downhill.

At one point he had to move through a patch of willows. It was the same place where Joyce and he had been snapped at by two snarling grizzlies on their first-ever fishing trip into the area. Jeremy hates willows, which he views as prime hiding spots for bears. He was shaking with fear as he crossed the stand of willows.

Jeremy knew that between him and the Turner outfitters' camp were several small, temporary camps set up by hunters who came in on horseback. That morning, on his bicycle, he had passed a camp where two hunters on horseback were staying beside a creek — it was their attention he had tried to attract when he fired off multiple rounds after the attack.

"I picked up the pace. It was such a relief they might be so close. If I could get there, they could haul me out," Jeremy remembers. What he couldn't remember was exactly which camp was theirs. He started hollering and firing rounds. He hoped they would be in camp when he got there. They were not, having moved out about 30 minutes before Jeremy's arrival.

"When no one was there, I broke down and started crying. I was heartbroken," says Jeremy. Now in tall spruce, shaded from the harsh sun rays, he felt it was safe to take off his sweater and hang it on overhanging branches between the creek and the trail junction to show he had been there in case the hunters returned.

His next goal was to reach the Turner camp. The great Alberta flood of 2013 had braided the creek into many small streams with what seemed like quicksand in between. A few days later, when Jim Turner came out to examine his outfitters' camp, he would be able to see markings in the creek sand where Jeremy had dragged his leg.

Finally, starving and thirsty, Jeremy reached the camp. He could barely see, but he had been drawn to the camp by the buzzing of the top and bottom wires of the electrified fence that surrounded it. He was exhausted, yet he managed to disconnect the two sets of wires and, once inside, reconnect them to keep bears away. Inside, he hoped to find a radio to summon help. Usually one was there, but not this time. The Turners had taken the radio and satellite phone with them to prevent theft.

He first went through the sleeping tent but found nothing of value he could use. In the main living tent, he tried to unlatch a supply cabinet, but his hands were too damaged. He tossed it to the ground, shattering the latch open. Inside he found a can of ham with a pull tab and a pocketknife. He was unable to open the can with either the knife or by pulling the tab, so he grabbed a second can and begin slamming them together until he could pluck out some food. In another container, he found two multi-pack boxes of juice and slammed several back. He found water bottles but could not open them even after crashing them against the dining table.

He rummaged through one of the supply drawers and found a roll of toilet paper and some veterinarian's tape used to treat injured horses. He wrapped his whole head in the toilet paper and then, fitting his jaw back in place, he wrapped his head in the vet tape, all the while continuing to bleed. He also used the vet tape on his leg using the x-style pattern he had learned playing football. He covered the holes in his hand with tape.

"My jaw was just hanging down. I put it back in position. It sort of clicked into place and I felt so much better," he remembers. "I could actually talk."

Out of energy, and cold, he pulled a sleeping bag out from beside the stove and laid it on the floor. He yearned to give up and just lie there and let things take their natural course. He had set the alarm on his phone to keep him awake. Every 30 seconds the alarm went off to remind him of his goal of seeing his wife and daughter again. Annoyed with the alarm and knowing that trail ahead was flatter and easier walking, he decided to trudge on.

Before leaving, he found a piece of paper and a permanent marker pen. Always a gentleman, considerate and respectful of the property of others, Jeremy wrote in large letters the following note: "Sorry was attacked by a bear, its really bad was looking for radio or sat phone sorry about the mess, my name is Jeremy Evans [cellphone number]."

Jim Turner and his son Jody — the 2003 Canadian bull riding champion — found the blood-smudged note on a table near the torn-apart veterinarian kit. There was blood everywhere. When they turned over the note, the hairs on the back of their necks curled. Jeremy had written: "I don't think I will make it. My wife is Joyce [her cellphone number]. Tell her I love her. I feel very weak. Loss too much blood."

Deciding he had come too far to give up, he continued the tough journey to his truck. Leaving the camp, he fired off his last three rounds, but no one came to his rescue. He reset the electric fence. Leaving his rifle behind and carrying the last five juice boxes, he hobbled off. His injured leg had stiffened; the vet tape helped, though, and at times he could walk awkwardly instead of just crawling. There was still about five miles to go, or about eight kilometres. His plan was to drink one juice box every mile, leaving each one behind to create a trail for searchers to find if he did not make it out. And that is what he did, rationing the juice boxes in an exacting pattern. He knew wildlife would devour him if he passed out along the trail.

About 500 metres from the outfitter camp is a large open field highlighted by two large spruce trees. Delusional, Jeremy thought the trees were two horses and a wagon coming for him. He could even hear the horses. "I got so excited and then I got very disappointed," he remembers.

At the final creek crossing, Jeremy had two options. Normally, he would head up the trail over the steep ridge — a tough climb in his current state, but he might run into incoming hunters who could help him. The other option was to walk down the creek — only two to three kilometres extra, and on flat terrain. But it could be washed out or full of deadfall. Jeremy had not taken that way out since the flood. The choice was clear now as he finished the second-last juice box and set it on the side of the creek. He made his way down the trail towards the ridge.

He took short steps up the steep climb. He knew this hill very well, and with each step he could picture how far up the hill he was. Even though he could not see well, he looked for a pair of remarkably familiar rocks that lay in the middle of the trail — they were the size of five-gallon pails, and Jeremy had always been too lazy to move them off the trail. To his surprise, the rocks were just feet way from him. Jeremy realized he had a single juice box left, the one that he was saving for the last section of the trail. But this seemed more fitting. He sucked it back and placed it on one of the rocks. He kissed his hand and touched both rocks: he now knew he was going to make it. The last stretch was downhill. He was less than a kilometre from the gate and his truck, although there would remain the drive to the Lodge at Panther River — a 16-kilometre route with hairpins and steep drop-offs.

Another obstacle was the gate itself. It was of uncomplicated design: two strands of metal pipe strung horizontally between two posts. The pipe was about three feet off the ground, to stop off-road vehicles from entering. Extending from each side of the gate was a four-foot-high chain-link fence that ran along the ditch perpendicular to the road to prevent off-roaders from going around the gate.

Jeremy spent considerable time trying to figure out how to get through the gate. He normally just walked his bike around the north side, but that meant traversing about 60 metres to get around the fence then 60 metres back to the road. On the verge of exhaustion, he was worried if he attempted to crawl under the gate, he would pass out and die. Ultimately, the decision was taken. He crawled under the pipe and started to pass out. He grabbed a sign on the gate and held on for dear life once again. "I was so dizzy I became disoriented," Jeremy remembers. The ten minutes he held on felt like forever.

Finally, he gathered sufficient strength to reach the truck, a vehicle that used a keypad lock. Jeremy worried his fingers would not be able to punch in the code. To his relief, the locks popped on his first try. He retrieved his keys and inserted them in the ignition. Before moving, he jammed the rear-view mirror to the side and moved the side mirrors out of position: he did not want to catch a glimpse of what he looked like. His right leg did not have sufficient strength to push the brake pedal, so he had to wiggle around to use his other leg.

To anyone who grew up driving the Panther Road, it's incredible that Jeremy, his eyes almost swollen shut and able to see only extremely blurry images, was able to avoid the precipices where the truck could easily have rolled several hundred feet down steep embankments. Even on the absolute best of days, it is a treacherous drive.

Jeremy drove very slowly, frequently with his head out the window, trying to pick up any spots of light on either side of the road to guide him. His theory was that light images meant road and dark images were trees. Luckily, he knew the road well. At one point all he could see was light, so he knew he was at an open field near a bridge. He gunned it over the bridge and up the steep hill. He also successfully navigated a 180-degree hairpin turn where multiple drivers had gone off the road.

The biggest challenge was finding the turnoff to the lodge, which is hidden by trees. Once he found an entrance and entered the parking lot, he tried three or four times to back in beside a jeep and red truck. After failing, he drove past the authorized personnel-only sign and straight to the front entrance of the lodge. The truck had arrived without a scratch.

CHAPTER 5

The Lodge at Panther River

IT HAD TAKEN JEREMY ABOUT AN HOUR TO REACH THE Lodge at Panther River, a lovingly cared-for family-owned resort with a main building, ten cabins and two campgrounds with 50 sites. Terry Safron and his wife, Laureen, bought the resort in 2002; the couple had been hunting the area since the 1980s. Panther River Outfitting dates to 1979. The parents like to say their three daughters grew up with river water in their veins and the mountains in their heart. Of that there can be no doubt.

When Jeremy arrived at the porch of the main building, he struggled up the stairs to the lodge entrance door. Inside, staff were busy preparing for a wedding that was to take place the next day on horseback, two days before the anniversary of Jeremy's own wedding. The bride and groom were expected to arrive in a couple of hours.

Terry and Laureen's daughter Amanda, who to this day is primarily in charge of the resort, was napping in her cabin. It was the day before her birthday. Laureen was in the office, doing paperwork. Nanny Jay Mathews, just 18 years old, was looking after Amanda's three boys in the great room, which also features a coffee shop.

While most seriously injured men and women might have leaned on the horn to immediately summon help, Jeremy did nothing of the sort. He did not want to cause a loud ruckus that might disturb other lodge guests. That would have been simply too impolite and unfair to his friends, the lodge owners.

It was Ryden, Amanda's 9-year-old son, who first spotted the bleeding mauling victim with a dangling right eye just outside the door. "I thought it was a prank. I thought he was dressed up in a costume for Halloween," remembers Ryden, now a young man who can easily manage a horse or a powerful dirt bike. "It was very scary. I was really scared."

Jay raced to Amanda's cabin to get her. Her face was white. She yelled that Amanda immediately needed to get to the main cabin. Halfway there, Amanda stopped abruptly, concerned that she had failed to put her shirt back on after rapidly awakening from her nap. Luckily, she had not.

Jeremy was seated at a table when she arrived. Her mom was squeamish at the sight of so much blood. Amanda ordered her to call 911 to get help, then got out the first aid kit. She wanted to get a STARS Air Ambulance to the lodge before Jeremy died. "He should already have been dead. He had lost so much blood," she recalls. It had been eight hours since the mauling.

Amanda was expert in the mountains. A tall, dynamic blonde, she had begun riding horses and hunting as a child. She started guiding paid elk hunts when she was 16, and to this day still guides for the lodge's biggest clients. A week earlier, she had taken eight backpackers into the backcountry to shoot a video. She has a detailed knowledge of the Panther Valley and the Burnt Timber drainage. The mountains, she says, are magical, and there is no other place on earth as beautiful. The region features the most rugged country you can imagine, including the hills and ravines Jeremy had to climb to survive. It was as if he was a machine, she says, not a human nearing death.

Amanda and her mother kept trying to get STARS on the phone, but the helicopter ambulance could not come to the resort. She was never told why. At one point, a land ambulance was dispatched from Caroline, about 100 kilometres away. It got lost. The 911 calls were totally frustrating, as dispatchers did not know where to send help. As the minutes ticked away, Amanda realized it was very unlikely help would arrive in time. She called her dad, Terry, who owns and operates an oil business north of Eckville, about two hours away.

Terry had always had a passion for flying, getting his first fixed-wing licence in 1982 before getting turned on to the thrill of flying helicopters. Back to flight school in 2004, he received his first helicopter licence, with mountain flying certification added in 2005. In 2011 he graduated with a commercial helicopter pilot licence. He regularly flew fellow outfitters and lodge guests into the mountains in his jet-black Bell 206 helicopter.

Amanda explained what had happened, and that it was impossible to get help despite all the telephone efforts. All she knew was that Jeremy had been severely mauled by a grizzly, most likely in Burnt Timber.

"How bad is it?" Terry asked his daughter.

"It's bad," she replied.

Terry immediately responded: "I am on my way."

No other questions. Nothing about would anyone pay or anything like that. Rural Albertans, especially those who know the calamity that lurks in the mountains, act first and maybe ask questions later. When a person needs help, rescue comes first.

Amanda realized they would have to get Jeremy down to the garage area, where there was a landing spot for her dad's helicopter. She cleaned the blood off the seats of Jeremy's truck as best she good. She told him that her dad was coming in his personal helicopter, although it would be some time — Terry had to drive to where he stored the helicopter and then fly to the lodge.

There was still considerable blood in the truck, but Amanda and her nanny — who helped move his bandages up to stem the bleeding — were able to get Jeremy into the front seat. He asked Amanda to grab him a Gatorade. He couldn't drink it because the lip of the bottle was too large to fit through the taped-up hole in his jaw. She raced back in and got a straw so Jeremy could quench his thirst. Then Amanda drove to where her dad could land.

Jeremy was leaned up against the garage, located maybe 100 metres from the Panther River. Amanda fell to her knees and started praying for him. Jay Mathews took over the watch as Amanda went back to the 911 call, hoping maybe the ambulance had found the correct road to the lodge. Jay would spend about 45 minutes with Jeremy, helping him drink and talking to him to keep him alive.

"He had the craziest sense of humour. It was amazing," remembers Jay. "He kept cracking jokes." Jay thinks Jeremy's calmness kept her calm. She had never seen anything like it in her life — not in the mountains, fishing, dirt biking. Never. "What he did has made me a much stronger person," says Jay.

The mauling took place in what Amanda views as her backyard. Horrific things, she says, can happen to the best. What Jeremy did afterwards to survive is almost legendary at the lodge, including that he told Jay he had survived for his wife and daughter. "Here he was, fighting for his life, and he was constantly apologizing for the damage he caused to the outfitter's tent. It was incredible that apologizing was so important in his condition," Jay says. Amanda recalls Jeremy jokingly chastising Jay for not taking him fishing, claiming it was a spectacular day to catch a few trout.

As they waited for the helicopter, two Alberta Fish and Wildlife officers pulled up at the lodge, one male and one female. Amanda found it strange, because they almost never came by the lodge. It was pure happenstance. They knew nothing about the mauling. She took them over to Jeremy and Jay. The male officer said not to touch him. Like Amanda's mother, he felt queasy. The female was much more engaged.

Just at that moment, Terry arrived in the helicopter. A tarp was thrown over the back seats to protect them from the dripping blood. Jeremy was able to walk to the helicopter, and the others helped him climb in. It took about 15 minutes. He started bleeding more profusely. The female officer jumped in front. Amanda joined Jeremy in the back, relieved to have a professional with them.

On the flight, Amanda thought she was going to lose Jeremy. He started dozing off. In a loud voice, she kept telling him to stay strong. They spent probably 30 to 35 minutes in the air.

When they arrived at the Sundre Hospital and Care Centre, nurses ran out with a gurney. A doctor almost got caught in the swirling tail rotor of the helicopter. The hospital was ready to handle Jeremy, having received a telephone call from the lodge that a private helicopter with a mauling victim was on its way. During that call, hospital staff were warned multiple times to be prepared for a horrific scene. Be prepared for what you are going to see. And the trained professionals at this small hospital were.

After they landed, Amanda watched in disbelief as a nurse, who wasn't that big, grabbed Jeremy out of the helicopter and lifted him directly onto the stretcher, showing remarkable strength. "I just grabbed him and manoeuvred him onto the stretcher," recalls that registered nurse, Chantal Crawford, who also operates a ranch with her husband. "It is what farm girls do. I wrestle horses and cows. I did what I had to do."

Chantal personifies excellence in rural health care. Born and raised in Sundre, she yearned to return to work in her hometown after graduating from nursing at Red Deer College. She was hired first as a nurse at the local hospital, where today she is the site manager, a clinical nurse educator and a director of the recruitment and retention committee.

She frequently leads seminars for new nurses and rural physicians. Three months before the mauling, she spoke to a group of rural physicians about why she became a nurse. "So, what does it take to be a nurse?" she asked them.

> Well, for starters you need a big bladder and a small stomach, because pee breaks are far and few between, and meals breaks are on the fly. So, if you meet those criteria, you're off to a good start.
>
> But seriously, nurses are amazing, and I believe that being a nurse is a calling: it is in our hearts. We are professionals with a high level of

education and knowledge. We are taught critical thinking skills, communication skills, patient assessment skills and how to manage complex illnesses, and develop care plans and protocols to assist patients in achieving their optimum health.

Nurses are also compassionate and empathetic, without judgment towards another person who is suffering. Nurses are respectful of their patients and treat them with dignity. Many people see nurses as a safe person and a support person. People trust us and will confide in us.

We make connections with people, and sometimes these connections will have a lasting impression on the patients; but a lot of the time it will also have a lasting impression on us as well.

This was certainly the case between Chantal and Jeremy. Neither will forget the impressions they made.

CHAPTER 6

Sundre to Foothills Hospital

IT HAD BEEN A RELATIVELY QUIET DAY FOR JAMIE ORR, an advanced care paramedic based at the fire station in Sundre. He and his partner Clark Cochran had transported a patient from the local hospital to the much larger Red Deer Regional Hospital Centre for medical tests, roughly a one-hour, ten-minute drive.

As they were finishing in Red Deer, the driver from another ambulance crew leaned out the window and asked: "What is going on in Sundre?" They had heard something about a grizzly bear attack and that the victim was going to be transported to the hospital by helicopter. With eight years' experience as an emergency medical technician and ten more as a senior paramedic, Jamie had been on bear attack calls before. Usually, he says, the injuries are not that serious. He would soon find out that was not the case this time — not by a country mile.

Jamie and Clark quickly headed back to their home base in case help was needed. They were refuelling their ambulance in Sundre when they saw a black helicopter coming in over their heads. They raced to the nearby hospital.

Minutes earlier, Dr. Jonathan Somerville, a young physician with a passion for rural medicine, was just finishing seeing patients for the day at a nearby clinic. Having grown up on a farm near Edmonton, he loved the variety of looking after people from cradle to grave. When the call came from the hospital asking for help from anyone available, he and two other doctors ran to the emergency ward. He was not even on call, but in rural Alberta, when help is needed, you come running. Dr. Somerville worked two shifts a week in the emergency ward, so he knew the inner procedures well. He had no idea what to expect as they wheeled the gurney out to the helicopter. At first glance, he was stunned.

"I had never seen anything like this in terms of facial injuries," recalls Dr. Somerville, who has seen his share of traumas caused by horse, quad and car accidents. Jeremy was a mess of soft tissue covered with his shirt and toilet paper and wrapped in tape. "He had lost a significant portion of his face." Although he was still bleeding extensively and barely able to see, the survival actions Jeremy had taken had caused significant clotting. For his part, Jamie Orr had only seen one incident of similar destruction in his long rural career. It was an attempted suicide: the victim shot himself directly in the face.

When Orr arrived in the emergency room after Jeremy's arrival, the scene was chaotic. Doctors were hard at work. After IVs were inserted, they began systematically working through their medical procedures, especially checking their ABCs — airway, breathing, circulation. When they went through his clothes to see if they could find an Alberta Medicare card to check his health history, Jeremy asked what they were doing. After receiving the explanation, he reeled off the nine-digit number by memory. The doctors were stunned.

A cast was put on the injured leg, and his arm was bandaged. The most important initial step was to stabilize Jeremy and protect him from drowning in his own blood. A tube was inserted down his throat to suction blood when necessary. The decision was taken not to begin treating his face, and especially not to unwrap the tissue paper and tape. Foothills Medical Centre in Calgary, 113 kilometres to the southeast, was a state-of-the-art trauma centre much better equipped to manage Jeremy once his vitals were fully stabilized. With Level 1 accreditation, it is the largest trauma centre in the region.

STARS was called again — this time by the hospital — to come fly Jeremy between hospitals. Again, STARS was busy and could not come for at least 75 minutes. Worry mounted they might lose Jeremy due to his traumatic blood loss. While medical staff worked, an officer from

Fish and Wildlife arrived to collect information and his clothes for scientific testing. Their investigation had begun.

Paramedic Orr was certain he could get Jeremy to Foothills by ambulance sooner than the delayed helicopter could. With Clark driving and Dr. Somerville with Orr in the back, they sped around winding corners and down the highway at 130 kilometres an hour. Dr. Somerville's initial job was to hold Jeremy's head as steady as possible. And that he did, with as much strength and concentration as he could muster while travelling at breakneck speed. He was worried that if Jeremy vomited the results would be devastating. Jeremy was still bleeding a lot, and so the doctor didn't want him to speak — by using his vocal cords, Jeremy could lose the use of his airway.

Throughout the ride, Jeremy and Orr communicated through hand signals. Orr was charged with monitoring Jeremy's vital signs and operating the suction to remove blood from his mouth when Jeremy gave the hand signal. He was certain Jeremy was running on adrenaline and in a state of shock, driven by an unwavering will to live. But Orr worried what would happen if Jeremy started to decompensate — would he stop fighting and die? Decompensated shock is the late phase of shock, in which the body's compensatory mechanisms are unable to maintain adequate passage of blood through the vessels to the brain and vital organs, and the blood volume decreases by more than 30 per cent.

During the ride, Jeremy refused all offers of painkilling analgesics, such as morphine or fentanyl. He was afraid that if he went to sleep he would never get up.

With sirens blaring and lights flashing, the ambulance arrived at Foothills in under an hour. Dr. Somerville was looking out the window when he saw an older woman peering in. She reacted in shock and alarm. Her hand went to her mouth. He was certain it was Jeremy's mother. (He was right — Jeremy's mother, Cindy, later confirmed that she was there as the ambulance arrived.)

Orr says the scene was absolute chaos when they arrived at Foothills. They had radioed ahead, and maybe a dozen paramedics, nurses and doctors were waiting to see the arrival. He recalls many others in the trauma room. Doctors whispered to other doctors that they had to see what was in the room. Jeremy said to Jamie: "Find my wife. Give her your number."

Orr is a consummate professional with years of trauma experience, yet even he became slightly emotional when he walked into the quiet room where Joyce and Abby were waiting with several other family members. "Seeing his baby girl and wife, I let out an unexpected sob and teared up. My voice quivered and it was hard to speak because I was trying to control my emotions," he says. "As soon as I left, I was fine again. In my line of work, for me at least, those types of calls are not emotionally distressing. They are adrenaline-inducing. I live for those types of calls. But seeing his family got me emotional for a few moments."

Dr. Michael Dunham was the trauma surgeon whose team would provide the initial treatment to Jeremy at Foothills Hospital. It had been a steady day so far, more routine than dramatic. Then he took the call from a doctor inside a speeding ambulance. A horrifically mauled victim was on his way in from Sundre. He learned Jeremy was breathing, had a pulse and an acceptable blood pressure despite his significant blood loss.

Dr. Dunham grew up in Calgary breathing medicine and watching his father treat injured patients. His dad was an old-school neighbourhood doctor and an emergency room physician. More than a few people were sewn up with sutures on the family's kitchen table.

Like father, like son. Long before he graduated in medicine from the University of Alberta in 1999, Mike knew he would be a surgeon. By 2004 he held general surgery certification from the University of Calgary, and two years later he had completed advanced critical care and trauma surgery training at the University of Miami in Florida.

Given the advance notice his team — anaesthetist and nurses — was fully prepared when Jeremy arrived and was wheeled into the surgical suite. What they weren't immediately prepared for was that Jeremy had had the wherewithal "to do a battlefield dressing in the forest," says Dr. Dunham, who had never seen anything like it before despite his years as one of six rotating trauma surgeons at the hospital. Given the severity of his injuries and blood loss, the surgeon remains flabbergasted that Jeremy had the presence of mind to dress his wounds. He was also surprised Jeremy was able to talk lucidly about what happened deep in the Burnt Timber forest.

The team swung into disciplined, well-practised and exacting action, once again checking the ABCs — airways, breathing, and circulation — while keeping Jeremy awake during intubation, the introduction of an endotracheal tube to ensure air could get to the lungs. It was sewn to his lip and would remain like that for hours of surgery. Two full CAT scans followed, primarily to check for major internal injuries to the lungs, heart and arteries or veins. Almost unbelievably, there were there no significant ones, not even a potential collapsed lung that had worried the surgeon.

Jeremy was then put to sleep so attention could be focused on the face, neck, skull, thigh and abdomen injuries. Slowly and painstakingly, they undid the veterinarian tape and tissue Jeremy had covered himself in — the aptly described "battlefield dressing." Although the eye itself was intact, Dr. Dunham recalls being able to see right through the interior socket wall. Jeremy's nose was attached by a thin thread of skin. There was also major wound contamination that had to be cleaned, and pine needles, parts of pine cones and even grizzly bear hairs that had to be removed. Work was also done on the ear. The degloved scalp, missing a piece of skin about 15 centimetres by 20 centimetres ripped off the skull, needed to be initially dressed before transfer to the plastic surgeon. Trauma treatment took more than two hours before Jeremy was transferred upstairs to the next operating suite.

Shortly before ten p.m., the plastics team began their work, the next step in treating Jeremy — a process that would ultimately involve more than 40 health care professionals. Throughout, Dr. Dunham was impressed by Jeremy's strength. "He was not upset with the bear," he says. "He just feels lucky." Dr. Dunham feels this is a story of man against the strength of nature, and Jeremy, despite being an exceptionally experienced outdoorsman, allowed the bear to get the drop on him. He could easily have died.

CHAPTER 7

Jeremy's Operations

Dr. Duncan Nickerson was the plastic surgeon on call that day. A veteran surgeon with specialized training in reconstructing victims of burn and traumatic injuries, he was called in from home by Dr. Dunham, arriving to start about ten p.m. Jeremy was already prepped under general anaesthetic and on the operating table. With a team of resident assistants, Dr. Dunham would operate for nine full hours, until seven the next morning.

"The extent of the facial injury was devastating," Dr. Nickerson wrote in his notes that night.

> There was a 15 x 15-centimeter area of full-thickness scalp loss in the right temporoparietal scalp. The right ear was destroyed with multiple complex lacerations. There was a transverse laceration cleaving the face at the junction of the right lower eyelid and cheek running transversely across the cheek and then the nose was

split vertically with the left half of the nose hanging on by just a thin strip of skin adjacent to the left nasolabial fold [the indentation line on the side of the mouth that extends from the edge of the nose to the mouth's outer corners].

The left cheek was transversely split similar to the right. There were lacerations of the left ear and the scalp posteriorly on the left side as well. The left globe [eyeball] was exposed. I am told that prior to induction of anaesthesia the patient confirmed that he was able to see out of the left eye. The orbital rim [eye socket], the nasal sidewall, the maxilla [bone that forms the upper jaw], the zygoma [cheekbone], and the arch of the zygoma were shattered into at least 8 main pieces.

Putting Jeremy back together was exacting, painstaking work, and the first of multiple operations Jeremy would have over the next few months. Imagine the idea of putting the pieces of a human jigsaw puzzle back together, except the pieces were Jeremy's face and scalp.

I began by reconstituting the skeletal framework of the left side of the face. Piecing this together from all the comminuted [pulverized] pieces, I felt that I would be able to restore the arch, the body of the zygoma, the nasal sidewall, and the infraorbital rim. It was clear that there would be somewhat of a deficit at the medial aspect of the infraorbital rim [meaning missing or damaged bone would need to be replaced by other materials].

Furthermore, it was evident that the buccal and frontal branches of the facial nerve would have been destroyed bilaterally and no repairable stumps were identified at this time. I began by forcing the frontal process of the zygoma to the zygomatic process of the frontal bone and in what appeared to be a reasonably anatomic position to reconstitute the lateral wall of the orbit [eye socket]. This piece carried on including the lateral portion of the infraorbital rim.

This was put on with a fairly flexible plate secured with just one incompletely tightened screw on either side of the fracture site to allow for adjustment. I then placed a long flexible plate from the stable part of the zygomatic arch posteriorly across an intercalated butterfly segment of arch onto the main body of the zygoma [cheekbone] and spanned this to the lateral buttress of the maxilla [upper jawbone]. Again, taking advantage of the fact that this is a fairly thin flexible plate with incomplete screws, we were able to adjust the configuration subsequently.

One of the main challenges was the segmental defect in the infraorbital rim centrally, and this was then spanned with a curvilinear plate up the nasal sidewall to the nasal process of the frontal bone [meaning a plate was used to replace areas of the skull that were missing or too damaged].

With some adjustment, I was able to achieve what appeared to be a very close to anatomic configuration [close to pre-injury] at which point the screws were tightened in the plates and the remaining screws were placed.

Another box-style plate was placed from the main body of the zygoma [cheekbone] up onto the main fragments consisting of the lateral component of the infraorbital rim. The body of the zygoma was then plated on to the medial and lateral buttresses as well. The wound was then once again thoroughly irrigated, and attention was turned to the soft tissue reconstruction. All the wounds had been debrided [damaged tissue and foreign objects removed]. All the wounds were closed ultimately using a combination of buried interrupted sutures of 4-0 Vicryl and 5-0 Monocryl and skin sutures of 4-0 nylon and 5-0 nylon. In the case of the more posterior scalp wounds, staples. The destruction of the right ear was impressive and at length. This was pieced back together and repaired using buried sutures of 5-0 Monocryl and 5-0 plain and chromic gut in the skin.

Doyle nasal splints [splints placed in the nostril] were placed in conjunction with packing to control nasal hemostasis [cessation of bleeding].

The missing segment of scalp was temporarily covered using a piece of dermal regeneration template stapled into the wound with a bolster dressing applied over top. Tarsorrhaphy sutures had been placed during the case, and these were now removed, and the eyes were thoroughly irrigated with balanced salt solution.

Attention was then turned to the left hand. There was a roughly a two-centimeter oblique palmar wound over the ulnar aspect of the palm and this was thoroughly irrigated and then packed open for subsequent attention at a subsequent operation.

There was a fracture of the left 5th metacarpal [bone within the hand connecting the pinky finger] confirmed with intraoperative fluoroscopy [x-ray], and a dosed reduction was undertaken followed by application of a well-molded, well-padded ulnar gutter splint with the intent being to return at a subsequent operation to engage in an open reduction and internal fixation of this fracture.

Jeremy was taken to the recovery room and later transferred to the intensive care unit. He had been registered under a fake name in case the story of his mauling and ultimate survival attracted media interest.

With 20 years' experience in plastic surgery, Dr. Nickerson comes across as a physician both exceptionally passionate and philosophical about his patients, especially the terribly scarred and traumatized ones treated at the Calgary Firefighters Burn Treatment Centre at Foothills, where he is the medical director.

Jeremy, he says, faced two main ongoing threats to his life — he could have become discouraged and simply given up, or he could have bled out, as the face is an extraordinarily rich blood supply. With his vast experience dealing with trauma victims, Dr. Nickerson says, "there is a whole range of behaviours people demonstrate." Some patients think something minor is the biggest challenge possible. Others blow what happened to them out of proportion. And then there are people like Jeremy. They are going to have a better outcome because of their positive attitude.

With his philosophical bent, Dr. Nickerson says everything in life is a choice, sometimes easy, sometimes much more tough. The Jeremys of the world would never think of taking the easy way. It was not engrained in his DNA — not then, not ever. His resiliency was powerful. His strength unquestionable. His love for wife and daughter as unbendable as a piece of steel. And his passion to return to the outdoors as soon as possible an unwavering motivator. "In this case," says Dr. Nickerson, "nature didn't win."

CHAPTER 8

Excerpts from Joyce's Diary

August 24, 2017

The day of the mauling started out as a fairly normal day
for me. I was helping Trout Unlimited Canada (TUC) with
water education kits. Volunteering with them had started
to become a semi-regular thing while on maternity leave
and I enjoyed helping them out. I kind of hoped for a job
there someday but finances are tough for non-profits.
Jeremy was out sheep hunting.

I showed up about 1 p.m. and worked until approximately 4:30 p.m. I noticed there was a WhatsApp call
from Jeremy at 3:34 p.m. Strange, I didn't even know he
had that app. I figured he maybe found cell reception on
top of a mountain. I tried to see if there was some sort
of message, but it was just showing as a "missed video
call." In retrospect, I wonder what I would have done if
I didn't miss the call in the TUC basement. I wish I didn't
miss the call.

It was time to head home and get our daughter, Abby, from my parents. I left the TUC office and there was a total clusterfuck on Ogden Road and Glenmore Trail with all the construction. I ended up getting confused (big surprise) and drove down Ogden to Blackfoot / 17th Avenue. There was heavy traffic and I guessed it was because of GlobalFest, the international fireworks festival.

I got a phone call on the way back while driving down 17th at 4:53 p.m. from an RCMP officer. I don't have his name. It is written down on an envelope somewhere. It showed up as "No caller ID." Normally I would not take such a call (let alone while driving) due to a possible "rich prince from Nigeria" scam scenario, but something seemed terribly wrong. I had no idea why I felt that way.

I never would wish this feeling on anyone when you get news that your loved one is seriously injured. It's like your heart has been ripped out. Sounds corny, but it's true.

He told me who he was, and that Jeremy had been attacked by a bear. Even that was hard to write down. This shit doesn't happen to us. It happens to other people you don't know, in the news, elsewhere. All I knew was that he was alive and was headed to the Sundre Hospital. He said I should call someone named Amanda at the Lodge at Panther River.

Terrified, I pulled into a parking lot. Guess that was smart, so I didn't crash my car. It was in a parking lot for people going to GlobalFest. I was certainly not supposed to be there. Some guy in a brightly coloured visi-vest looked over at me and must have observed my distress so he left me alone. Good thing.

The next hour or so was a whirlwind of phone calls which consisted of notifying family, trying to get a hold of Amanda, calling Sundre Hospital, etc. I managed to get a doctor from Sundre on the phone and he described Jeremy's condition. Hope. His vitals were stable, and he was conscious and coherent. Apparently, he could recall his Alberta health care number. The doctor said that half his face was gone. Gone! What a word to describe someone's face. That was very distressing to me to think what he was going through. I knew I would love him no matter what and I just wanted to see him, squeeze his hand and tell him it was going to be ok. I had to get to him.

I have no idea how I drove myself home without crashing. Glad I did. He wouldn't have appreciated defying the very laws of what a human is capable of just to have me die or get hurt in a lame car accident.

We learned he was going to the Foothills hospital. My parents drove me with Abby, and I remember them having trouble finding the parking area and me screaming, of course. Jeremy's younger sister Jessica, her husband Matt, and Jeremy's mom Cindy beat us there. Jeremy's older sister Jennifer also arrived. I came in and Jessica took my hand to go see him. She said, "it's not pretty." I was scared but needed to see him.

What I am about to describe I will never forget my whole life. Despite the horror, it was actually quite fascinating. He was lying down, and we only had about 30 seconds to see him. This is the kind of shit that happens in movies, not to me. Mostly I just saw gauze/bandages. Essentially there was a lot of red where the bandages weren't covered. I later learned that Jeremy was adamant I didn't see his face. Above his right eyebrow there was a chunk of flesh missing and I could see his skull. Something white. Below his eye was just red.

That is not what I stared at, though. What I saw was the eye of a survivor, a fighter, full of life. His eye was bright green in a sea of red. The contrast was shocking, like a bolt of electricity. I later learned a Sundre nurse had a similar comment. I forgot how breathtakingly beautiful his eyes were. It was my favourite part about him, and I had almost forgotten. When was the last time I stared into his eyes? Like really gazed, like we did when we were teenagers? Why didn't I do that anymore? When life gets so busy, you forget all the precious things.

It wasn't just the stunning colour of his eyes alone. It is that he was still there. I knew it would be ok then. I was scared, but seeing him meant the world to me. We exchanged a few words. He said he was sorry. Like he was in trouble? Like we had a fight, and he was finally apologizing? I don't know why he said that. I said something of the sort that there was nothing to apologize for, thank you for coming back to us and I love you. He was then taken away, too soon, to go into surgery for facial reconstruction. He also asked about Abby.

That night was just waiting for his surgery to be done. Jessica, his younger sister, had handed me his wedding ring. It was covered in blood, and she washed it off for me. Everyone else but me and his mom went home. My boobs got really full and sore, as I was still nursing Abby. In retrospect I should have just gone home.

I think about that moment when I saw him before surgery 24/7. All I can think of is a green eye surrounded by red. That will never go away.

August 25, 2017

I finally left the hospital at about 5:30 a.m. when we were told it was going to be another three hours of surgery. I got zero sleep. My mom set me up on her couch, but I didn't sleep. She had a crib set up for Abby down there too. I think I just stared at old photos of Jeremy.

We got word he was done surgery and we all headed back. He was in the intensive care unit still sedated with a breathing tube. Slowly they took away the sedative so he could wake up. He was starting to stir. I was scared he was going to rip out the breathing tube. Dave, his older brother, said someone once ruined his vocal cords doing that in a panic.

He came to and gave lots of thumbs up. That was pure Jeremy. He hated the breathing tube. It came out and he was immediately relieved. His face looked amazing compared to how his injuries had been described. I was so relieved, as I was expecting worse. The doctor was pleased with the results.

At one point Jeremy asked me if I would still love him with all the scars. At that point, he had no idea how he looked. I was going to say, "it's a face I could sit on," thus quoting a Deadpool movie, but Jennifer, his older sister, was nearby and I figured that was inappropriate.

I had a phone call that evening from a fellow who was leading the Fish and Wildlife investigation from Alberta Environment and Parks. I remember being quite concerned over media or social media harassment, as people online can be terrible. Since Jeremy is a hunter, I wasn't sure if the "anti hunters" and such would come harass us or something (remember the "Cecil the lion" incident with the dentist), especially if the bear ended up being destroyed. Again, that night I slept at my parents' house with Sammy (my dog). I talked to my friend Shona, which was comforting.

CHAPTER 9

Jeremy's Surgery Continues

TWO DAYS LATER, ON AUGUST 27, JEREMY WAS BACK in the operating room. The goal of the surgery that day was to deal with his knee, repair the fractured pinky finger where part of the bone had been pulverized, and undertake a skin graft of his exposed skull with tissue harvested from his hip. Doctors spent time explaining the various procedures to Jeremy and obtained his informed consent.

Once again Dr. Nickerson was the primary surgeon. Jeremy was brought to the operating room and placed supine on the operating room table. After the placement of appropriate leads and monitors, and after the completion of a World Health Organization Surgical Safety Checklist, the general anaesthetic was administered.

First up for treatment was the knee. The right lower extremity was prepped and free draped. There was a complex wound on the knee where the bear had clawed him during the mauling and the hand-to-hand battle that ensued. The following description of what took place in the operating room that day is based primarily on Dr. Nickerson's medical notes.

The injury was essentially a transversely oriented internal degloving connected underneath the surface, but with three different surface lacerations. Degloving, also called avulsion, is a type of severe injury that happens when the top layers of your skin and tissue are ripped from the underlying muscle, connective tissue or bone. It can affect any body part, but it's more common in the legs and other extremities. Degloving injuries are often life-threatening.

One of the wounds was lateral, towards the side of the knee and about two centimetres long. One was medial, towards the middle of the knee and about two centimetres long. The dominant central portion of the wound was essentially across the whole knee and at the level of the tibial tubercle, just above the shin bone where the tendon is attached.

The areas around the wound were thoroughly debrided with all damaged tissues removed. The wound was subjected to copious irrigation. Hemostasis, the cessation of bleeding, was achieved. A suction drain was exited through the lateral wound, and then three wounds were closed in layers using buried sutures. A bulky supportive dressing was applied.

Attention was then turned to the left upper extremity, where the hand was prepped and free draped. The wound on the palm was copiously irrigated and explored.

Fortunately for Jeremy, no flexor tendon or digital nerve damage was found. After thorough irrigation and debridement, the wound was closed.

Surgical focus then turned to the dorsum, or back of the hand. A scalpel incision was made along the pinky finger, revealing a fracture of the metacarpal with sufficient pulverization that anatomic reduction (returning the bones to their original positions) was not possible. Generally, for the fractured bone to heal without any deformity, the bony fragments must be re-aligned to their normal anatomical position.

Dr. Nickerson believes, however, that near anatomic reduction was achieved despite some challenges. "A s-hole plate from the 2 mm component of the Synthes modular hand plating system was applied using appropriately depth gauge measured screws with 2 screws, bi-cortical, distal to the fracture site, and 2 bi-cortical screws proximal to the fracture site," he wrote. "Two attempts were made to get the position of the proximal screws just right to minimize any angulation at the fracture site. Good bony apposition was achieved, but as mentioned, the best possible reduction was not perfectly anatomic due to loss from comminution."

The finger was checked to ensure that there was no gross malrotation, meaning it could grow out of rotational alignment with another bone. The wound was thoroughly irrigated. And then Dr. Nickerson closed and dressed the wound.

Attention then turned to repositioning Jeremy on his left side to allow unfettered access to the right side of the scalp and the right ear. The right ear had previously been debrided and closed, but there was some further tissue necrosis. Dr. Nickerson knew this was unsurprising, given the level of contamination and the level of shredding of the ear skin. This was now debrided again and loosely reclosed with sutures.

Earlier, a skin graft for the scalp had been harvested from the right thigh, and the donor site dressed. The scalp wound that had been previously dressed was debrided, and the graft was affixed to it with staples. A bulky bolster dressing applied to the grafted areas was itself also affixed directly to the scalp with staples. Jeremy was awakened, extubated and taken to the recovery room in good condition.

Jeremy says about the only difference between his pinky today and before the mauling is that it doesn't bend like it did before. Sometimes it sticks out and gets caught on things, but he is used to that now. Most important, it does not impact his casting while fly-fishing with his wife and family.

CHAPTER 10

More Excerpts
From Joyce's Diary

August 27–30, 2017

August 27 is our anniversary. We got married in 2011 and have been together since 2002. He wished me happy anniversary while in the ICU and high on pain medication. He needed a blood transfusion. I recall he was looking really pale, cold and very lethargic so I told an ICU nurse and they brought blood. Apparently, we have the same blood type (B+). I wanted to donate my blood, but they had some. Jeremy ate some solid food for the first time, vegetable soup and mashed potatoes. His friend Wayne Brennen was around a lot. It was great to have him around, as he is a comforting presence to Jeremy. He is seven or eight feet tall (not actually but really tall), kind of intimidating with a loud booming voice. He is very protective of Jeremy, kind of an older fellow who is a father figure to Jeremy perhaps.

I keep thinking about the green eye with the red. I almost got out of bed one night and drew a picture. I thought about cutting up my own face so I knew how he felt but I for sure wouldn't do that. He would be pretty pissed. I had discussed some of my disturbing feelings with Patty (Wayne's wife).

I cannot recall exactly what day he came out of ICU and got moved to the burn unit at Foothills. One night I remember having to pump milk in the hospital room. Initially someone stayed with him almost all the time, as he was having severe nightmares/flashbacks. Jennifer, his older sister, stayed a few times overnight. I made and brought some origami fish and stuck them to the wall at the hospital room. He loves fish. I recall becoming worried about how home life would be after this, as he can get quite grumpy when sick/injured.

Jeremy was plagued by nightmares and there was nothing I could do. He said rubbing his feet is comforting. I pretended that I had some kind of healing magic I could transfer by touch.

During one of these days, he got a second surgery which was a skin graft and further repair to an ear. Skin grafting sounds horrible. They took skin off his thigh and then slapped it on the missing scalp part, I guess.

The nights alone were hard at home. I missed him so much it was like I was going to die of the hurt. I didn't sleep well, and Abby woke up at night anyway. Her presence and warmth while feeding were comforting.

Sometimes I texted Jennifer, his older sister, who was there at the hospital overnight sometimes, to see how things were.

August 31, 2017

Today marked a week since the attack. Jeremy is doing amazing. He is so strong. He sat up all on his own and I was super impressed. I think he is just happy to be alive. His vision is fine, but he reports seeing double sometimes. His eyes often don't move together which was due to muscle damage. So many positives in a situation that could have been far worse, including total blindness. Tomorrow he will stand, and I can't wait to see it.

I just love him so much. I keep telling him that. I'm probably being annoying. I find I can't find anything to say. He is either bored or really tired. I hope it's the latter. He is just so amazing.

Now he has to pee in a bottle as they removed his catheter. I think he is happy that it still works. Some face sutures were removed today, and he was such a trooper. I firmly rubbed his feet the whole time.

Writing in my journal I know I should go to bed. I hope Abby lets me sleep. She is cuter every single day. Love her so much and miss Sammy too (the dog). Feel terrible being away from Abby so much and at the hospital. Miss Jeremy so much it hurts so bad.

September 1, 2020

Drove myself to the hospital today. Said goodbye to Abby. Checked in with Jeremy quick then went to go purchase a parking pass.

The parking office was at least 10 miles away (not literally). What a weird location for that. It was in the basement. Generally, Foothills hospital is confusing. I thought of that Robin Williams comedy skit about GPS. Coming back to the burn unit, and holy shit he is in the hallway walking with a walker! It's an amazing thing to see him walking already about a week after the attack only.

His face looks great. He isn't ready to see it yet. Modern medicine is wonderful. They removed the bandage on his head where there was lost scalp. The amount of trauma a human can endure is surprising. Looks disturbing there and I think about when I first saw him. His ear also looks just fine, just swollen. Actually, I was expecting way more swelling than there was. Some pussing in places which is pretty gross.

Dr. Lindsay Friesen, a psychologist, comes by and was quite helpful and good for Jeremy and is helping with the flashbacks/nightmares.

His back seems to be reacting in a rash to the bedding or maybe just from sweating. Gave him a long massage, so now he is probably milking it! Really nice to start to see him back to his old self.

The evenings are hardest. Miss him, wish this didn't happen. How many times did I just go to bed, playing on my phone without even looking at him? When he comes home, so many things will change. There were days I barely even looked at him when he came home from work. Going back to our relationship, there were times I complained a lot or stewed about the negatives. We got along rather good for the most part since Abby was born, despite some past issues. Not rocky at all. Just there were so many lost opportunities when I could have kissed him at the door, smiled more, snuggled up close in bed, initiated intimacy, etc. He still thought the world of me no matter what. Maybe it was mostly Abby. Doesn't matter, I guess.

Apparently massage therapy improves overall body function, according to a nurse. Jeremy even asked the nurse for a massage therapist! The previous day, Jeremy's sister Jessica painted his toenails red, and he was the talk of the burn unit.

September 2, 2017

Today was not a hugely eventful day. While the head bandage was changed, Cindy (Jeremy's mom) had to leave. I took a better look this time. The whole time during the bandage change we discussed with the nurse how fun it is to pop zits. Jeremy did so well and didn't flinch.

The head wound was easier to look at and I can see how normal he will look when things heal. Now he has lots of fluid built up in his face in various places and it is making him very uncomfortable and dizzy. The nurse was squeezing some fluid out (super gross) which made him feel better. The swelling seems to be impacting his vision. He was explaining that he sees double at certain distances. The fluid is moving around in his face, which he can feel.

Feeling sad tonight. I decided to write down some positives:

- he is alive,
- no brain damage or organ damage,
- he can see,
- he can walk,
- getting better every day.

Nurse today looked and sounded like Alex from *Orange is the New Black*.

September 3, 2017

Today was a decent day. The ladies from the Lodge at Panther River came down to visit (Amanda and Jay). It must have been so traumatic for them to witness. When describing his injuries, I realized I never want to look at the selfie photo. Again, modern medicine is wonderful.

Both of them were beautiful and I'd be lying if I said I wasn't a little bit jealous. If I had been there, I probably would have been useless. The younger woman was very relieved to see his face. I am glad she came. Just thinking of me at 18 and trying to deal with what she had gone through, I was totally impressed. Miss him so much, as usual.

September 4, 2017

Jeremy has his phone now. Wish he would text me, but he is probably sleeping. He seemed unhappy when I left and told me not to text him. Anyways, I was reading about ICU stays and bedrest. Apparently, people lose 3–10% of their muscle mass a day in bedrest. Those are people that don't move at all and are sedated.

Go to sleep child! Abby has been up a million times a night and usually I give up and take her into bed with me. It is probably because she isn't nursing as much during the day while I am away at the hospital.

Oh, he texted me that's better.

So, muscle loss in hospital stays is a big deal, I guess. I read accounts from people online and how they couldn't even sit up. Anyways guess I'll play some Nintendo DS then go to bed. Jeremy did a long walk today down a bunch of hallways. Not sure why I am feeling anxious tonight.

September 5, 2017

Well, this notebook sucks (falling apart). Dollar store. Jeremy went on nine walks today. He is getting bored. Probably sick of the hospital and being poked and prodded. He is being such a trooper, so proud of him.

The skin graft donor site is bugging him, and it looks very painful. Wish I could have donated skin to him to save him the pain. We spent the day while I was there playing cards or going on walks. This evening I brought him some underwear, a Star Wars Lego set and a Nintendo DS game. Something to entertain him. He suggested the Lego since we can build it together.

He has had no nightmares since Friday evening when he kind of collapsed while standing when he had a flashback. He didn't fall down. I think Dave, his brother, sort of caught him. He gets dizzy from the fluid moving around. Lots of fluid comes out around his ear and the nurses flush it out with saline. As much as I'd like for him to come home, I would not feel comfortable caring for his wounds. Mammals aren't my specialty.

Amanda said her son beat off some wasps when they had clients at the lodge, and he says he wants to be just like the Grizzly Dude. It was a phrase Ryden coined. I feel like I am falling in love all over again. Everyone is going on about how amazing he is, and he is all mine.

September 6, 2017

Having a rough day and not exactly sure why. The feeling started when Jeremy said he needed some more surgery. Unfortunately, the doctor comes and talks to him early in the morning when I am not there, and I am not sure if he really pays attention. Something about drains in his face and additional skin grafting. Sounds awful. He has been doing so good with moving around and walking that more surgery would mean bedrest for a few days. It seems like a step back when I know it isn't.

I am having irrational thoughts. I often do anyway at the best of times. Seems like he perks up when he has other visitors but not with me. I can't help but feel like he doesn't want me around. Rationally, I know that isn't true. I think he puts on a bit of a show when others come and acts tougher. Then he is exhausted after when it's just me. But, of course, I would just worry that he doesn't like me. We were playing with Lego and focusing on the little Lego pieces and the instructions were hard for him to read (due to eyesight troubles) so he needed to rest. But it still makes me sad.

I just want more than anything to be able to snuggle and kiss him. He is still too fragile. It is such a shock when things change so fast. When your normal is so drastically ripped away and the nights are so lonely. I remember being excited to have the bed to myself when he went sheep hunting.

Find myself worrying about the future tonight. I was reading about marriages falling apart after one person is severely injured. These were usually much more serious things such as brain injury, leg amputation, paralysis, etc. I have no idea how I find the worst things to read. The internet is full of negativity. I don't actually think our marriage will fall apart or anything, just worried about change. I hate and fear change. Will intimacy be the same anymore? I don't mean because of his scars, as they don't bother me, and he is still attractive. I mean his mental state. Will he ever want me again?

On a happier note, he walks without the walker and just uses the cane that I brought. He can bend his leg more. It hurts but he is doing good. He walked all the way to the psychology office with Wayne and myself to make an appointment. He can also walk to the bathroom himself.

September 7, 2017

I am too tired to write much. I had a really bad day. Just feel like I've had enough of this nightmare, and I'd give anything to have things return to normal. They couldn't get an IV in him and he had to go for an emergency surgical IV insertion called a PICC (peripherally inserted central catheter). The morning was chaos and I'm finding it hard to cope.

Not even sure what else to say. I hope tomorrow is a better day.

September 8, 2017

Turns out today was a better day. Jeremy looked in the mirror today for the very first time and he seemed all right with it. He'd thought it was much worse. The surgeons did an incredible job, and he was relieved. Apparently, he thought he looked like Deadpool. Dr. Friesen, the psychologist, convinced him to look. He also did some stairs today and had no issues with it. Doing really well and enormously proud of him. He still looks great with scars, and I can't wait until he can be at home.

The man that owns the outfitter tent (Jim Turner) had come by the previous night. He brought the note. A small piece of paper about 6″ by 4″. The paper is lined, and he wrote with black Sharpie. There are large drops/smears of blood. The note should be horrifying but I find it special that he thought to write about me.

Some friends came over today which was nice. Wayne, his tall friend, made Abby a matching "hat" (head dressing) and we took pictures of her and Jeremy.

September 9, 2017

It was another pretty good day. Jeremy built some Lego without too much trouble. The Fish and Wildlife guy in charge of the investigation (Todd) brought the rest of Jeremy's stuff today. They talked for a while and Todd had photos of the scene. He emphasized making sure bear spray is always accessible.

I forgot to mention yesterday that Jeremy put on real clothes. Today he went outside for the first time. He was a little wary of the shrubs and trees around the hospital.

He is supposed to get more surgery but not sure when and not sure exactly what. Whenever he tells his story I can't believe this amazing person is mine. I feel either devastated about what happened and what he had to endure or high on being in love and obsessed with him. Like when I was 15 and my heart fluttered when I looked at him.

September 10, 2017

Not much going on today. A few visitors came by. The antibiotics are giving him headaches and making him dizzy. I went to Patty and Wayne's today for a bit, just a short visit.

I spent the night looking for pictures of him on all our computers (3 laptops and 1 desktop). Turns out there are hardly any that aren't hunting or fishing (big surprise!). I finally found a good one from our wedding photos. The lighting is good and it's a close up. Can see his eyes good. It is something to stare at when I'm not with him. I guess I should have taken more photos of him.

FROM TOP Alberta Fish and Wildlife spent several hours searching the North Burnt Timber drainage for the attack site; the huge bull trout Jeremy and Don Logan caught on their bike trip five days before the mauling.

FROM TOP Jeremy's Specialized Rockhopper mountain bike, which he used to fend off initial attacks, was tossed up a hillside into trees and shrub by the grizzly; after the attacks Jeremy scattered his pack in the hope it would be more easily seen by searchers.

Spent shells, Jeremy's favourite candy, and bear scat at the spot where he was attacked before firing randomly at any dark shape he could see.

The Turner outfitters' camp.

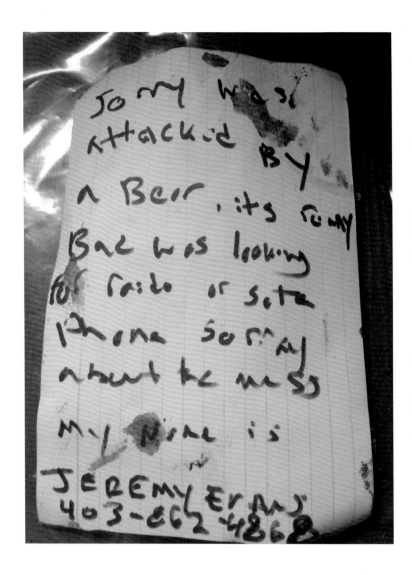

Side one of the handwritten note Jeremy left while looking for a phone at outfitters' camp.

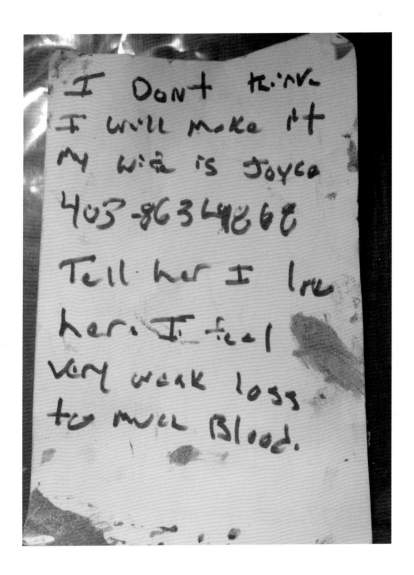

On side two of the blood-smudged note, Jeremy tells Joyce he loves her and isn't likely to make it out.

Photo taken by Jeremy immediately
following the mauling.

The trail gate fence Jeremy could not decide how to cross to get back to his truck.

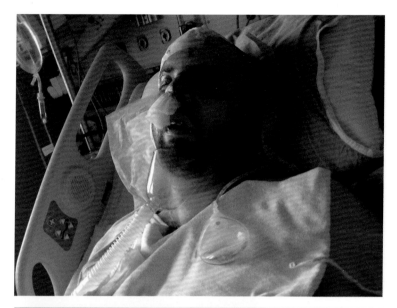

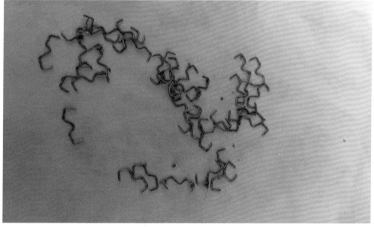

TOP Jeremy recovering after nine hours of facial reconstruction surgery.

BOTTOM Staples removed from Jeremy's skull.

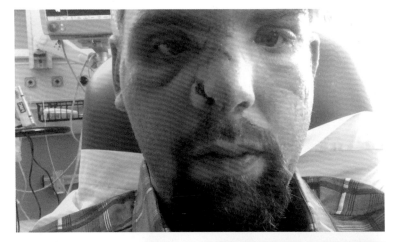

ABOVE Jeremy's first time looking in the mirror after his surgery.

RIGHT Jeremy's scalp and skull healing slowly, even with transplanted skin.

Jeremy at the shooting range on his first day pass from hospital.

Alberta Fish and Wildlife officers fly a bear trap in to the attack site.

Jeremy with a mule deer harvested on a Hutterite colony the November after the mauling.

Jeremy and Don Logan haul sheep up a steep mountainside for harvesting.

ABOVE A year after the attack, during his first return to the site, Jeremy walked to the drainage he had tumbled down into the boulders below.

FACING PAGE, TOP Family photo, October 2021: Jeremy, Joyce, Abby and Toby.

FACING PAGE, BOTTOM Plastic surgeon Dr. Duncan Nickerson and resident Dr. Jennifer Redwood with Jeremy after the operations.

Sign on the Panther River Road.

CHAPTER 11

Yet Another Operation

ON SEPTEMBER 22, JEREMY HEADED BACK TO THE operating room again. Overall, most of his injuries had healed fairly well, according to the doctors who examined him, although the left eyelids, both upper and lower, had been completely denervated by the trauma — they lacked strength and were largely non-functional. He was using eyedrops to protect his cornea.

However, while skin grafting had been successful for much of the large scalp wound, there were two areas, each measuring about one centimetre by two centimetres, of exposed skull that would not be amenable to grafting. Claw marks were discovered right in the bone of the skull itself.

Dr. Nickerson, the plastic surgeon who had pieced together Jeremy's face, felt that an appropriate way to address the situation was to take part of the existing healthy scalp and use it to cover the two affected areas where the bone was exposed. By transposing the scalp to cover the exposed bone, he could potentially return the flap to its original donor site later, after the area healed, and begin tissue expansion to restore hair-bearing skin. After the relevant merits and risks were outlined by the surgeon, Jeremy made the decision to proceed with the operation.

Once again, he was brought to the operating room and placed supine on the operating table. His head was placed on a horseshoe headrest to allow complete access to as much of the scalp as possible. His hair had been shaved.

"We began by mapping out a posteriorly-based transposition flap of adequate width to cover the area of exposed bone on the right temporal fossa region. The scalp defect was thoroughly debrided," wrote Dr. Nickerson in his post-operative notes. "The transposition flap was elevated, leaving the pericranium behind so that it could be skin grafted. The flap was viable with excellent bright red bleeding from its leading edge. It was of an excellent color."

The flap was transposed and inset into the defect it was intended to cover. A skin graft was harvested from the right thigh and applied to the remainder of the wound where there was exposed bone. A small piece was also applied to a secondary wound about two centimetres in diameter on the left side of the skull that had failed to heal after the original trauma. The skin graft was also applied to the donor site that the transposition flap had been taken from and inset using staples.

And then something went terribly wrong.

"At this point, it became obvious that the flap had become venous congested in the process of transposing it. It was a fairly deep purple in color and was already beginning to exhibit petechial hemorrhage at its distal portion," wrote the surgeon. "Accordingly, it was felt that the safest thing to do was to treat today's surgery as a 'delay' procedure... The inset of the flap was taken down, and it was transposed back to its original donor site and inset there using staples where its color immediately began to improve."

Basically, the surgeon thought Jeremy's body could not tolerate the challenge of having all of its venous drainage through the posterior base of the flap, at least not when the operation was taking place. The venous system is composed of venules and small and great veins, which serve to return blood from tissues to the heart. The systemic venous system brings deoxygenated blood from tissues and organs back to the right atrium of the heart, whereas the pulmonary venous system brings oxygenated blood from the pulmonary circulation back to the left atrium of the heart.

Dr. Nickerson believed that after maybe a week to ten days of preconditioning of the skin flap back in its original donor site, the surgical team might be able to re-transpose it during a subsequent operation. A skin graft was placed over the relevant area of the skull and a bulky bolster dressing applied to the entire scalp, followed by a burnnet-style head dressing. Jeremy was awakened, extubated and taken to the recovery room in good condition.

Later that afternoon, Dr. Nickerson met with Jeremy and his wife on the ward to explain the unexpected events of that day's surgery. He indicated that when the five-day bolster dressing came off, he would assess the skin graft and determine whether future surgical intervention was required. The skin graft, he explained, had only a 10 per cent chance of success in addressing the exposed skull areas. However, he gave Jeremy an extra 2 per cent for being so hardcore.

It didn't matter. Jeremy had had enough. "It did not work, so they were going to do the tissue expanders and try again if the skin graft did not work," Jeremy recalls. "I turned down the option to move the hair around on my head. I was tired of the pain and all that."

The skin graft did work well, covering most of his scalp, despite the odds. To this day, Jeremy has a portion on the front right side of his head where no hair grows or will ever grow. But he can live with that.

CHAPTER 12

Foothills Reflections

FIVE DAYS AFTER THE FAILED SCALP OPERATION, DR. Nickerson reviewed the skin graft he had placed over most of the remaining damaged skull area. If the graft had taken well, he would let Jeremy go home. Doing so, he felt, would allow Jeremy's excellent progress to continue. Alternatively, if the skin graft had failed, he knew Jeremy would have to stay in hospital for yet more operations.

The news was positive. Early that evening, Jeremy was discharged. He had been in the hospital for just over 36 days. Joyce was told it would be six months to a year before he could return to work. It was likely to be a very lengthy rehabilitation.

Little did they know Jeremy and his fierce determination to get on with his life. Two weeks later, seven weeks after the mauling, he was back to work full time. And within a month he was biking to work, 12 kilometres each way, every day, in winter.

When Jeremy recalls his hospital stay, he remembers the terrifying nightmares, but also the cherished time spent with family and friends, the great staff who cared for him in such a professional, kind manner, and time spent planning his next sheep hunting trip. He remembers waking up on day one to his wife's presence. He couldn't really see her, because his eyesight at the time amounted only to blurry images. It would stay that way for a considerable time. But awaking that first day, he could feel Joyce's warmth and hear her voice, something he came dangerously close to losing forever in the North Burnt Timber Forest.

It would be months before any semblance of quality eyesight would begin to be restored, and even today, having lost his tear ducts during the mauling, he frequently has water buildup in the eyes, especially when it is windy. His eyelids still have little movement.

After the second major operation within three days of the mauling, Jeremy was being moved from the intensive care unit to the burn unit when he asked what day it was. When he didn't know and was told the date, he said, "Gosh, it's my anniversary." As he would later recall, "It was not the way I had hoped to spend my wedding anniversary." Joyce was waiting when he got to the room, while his younger sister, Jessica, argued with the charge nurse that he needed a private room, not a double one. Fortitude and strength must run in the family, because within two hours he was moved into a private room. Joyce spent most of that night there, as she would many nights.

Jeremy spent much of the time cracking jokes about his own predicament and making the hospital staff smile. After the second major operation, a nurse asked him how his pain level was, and he replied, "Unbearable."

On September 1, only days after the mauling, staff got Jeremy, his head still massively wrapped in bandages, up on a walker. The goal they set for him was to try to move the length of the bed. But Jeremy was no laggard. Once he got up the head of steam, down the hallway he ambled. He almost made it to the nursing station, a distance of more than 60 feet. He will never forget the magical, surprised look on Joyce's face as she stepped out of the elevator and saw him moving.

A day earlier, he had again surprised her when she found him sitting up in bed, feeding himself. This, Jeremy says, represented a major step in his recovery because, before that, he had to be served baby food — all that he was allowed to eat — by the nurse or other hospital staff. Those meals left Jeremy hungry, so his older brother, Dave, went to the grocery store to purchase a load of baby food. With his help, Jeremy devoured it.

One of his visitors was Todd Ponich, a team leader with Alberta Fish and Wildlife. A veteran with 34 years experience, he has taught wildlife human attack training across North America and was heading the investigation into the mauling and a multi-officer effort to trap the grizzly so it could be euthanized, as directed by Alberta government policy. The initial meeting was spent interviewing Jeremy about what happened — a story Jeremy would repeat many times to many different people.

That day, Jeremy, Todd and Joyce walked outside the hospital. It marked the first time Jeremy had been outside since the mauling and Joyce remembers Jeremy being fearful of what animals might be lurking behind trees.

During the hospital stay, Joyce and Jeremy sent each other several lengthy and emotional notes, as they had during their courtship. In one, Jeremy describes his journey out to his truck after tumbling down the drainage and crashing into the rocks below. Following are some excerpts:

> I finally got enough courage to get up and read your note. Sorry it took so long. I just was not ready. I am sorry you had to see me like that. Man did I feel bad. I wish you were on holidays, and you never knew what happened. I feel so bad for putting you through all this. You deserve much better. Everyone calls me a hero or super tough. Well, I am not. In actual fact, I gave up on the mountainside. I found a nice stump and lay against it waiting to pass on.

> The only reason I started to walk out to the main trail was to make it easier to find my body. It was when I fell down the rocky drainage that things really set in. I could not move I was in so much

pain. I pulled out my phone looking at pictures of you and Abby. I could not see very well but was daydreaming of being with you guys in the kitchen sticking your tongues out.

Baby Shark came on and it was tough to just lie there. It was at that moment I decided I could at least try to get out. I owe you at least that much. Then I stopped thinking how far I had to go. And to just crawl to the next rock, and then the next. I slowly made my way up to the trail. The whole time I was playing Baby Shark. Man was that a long walk. Every step, I could not stop thinking about you and Abby. I just wanted to hear your voice.

So thankful I have someone like you in my life. I don't know why people call me their hero. A hero saves people. All I did was save myself. You are the true hero!! You saved my life more than once. If not for you I would still be out there. You sit beside my bed every day keeping me safe. Making me comfortable. I don't know how to thank you for all this. You are my hero. When I get out of here, I am going to be a better man. Family comes first from now on.

There can be no doubt the mauling, as horrific as it was, strengthened their relationship. Joyce responded with her own strength after she had read Jeremy's note. Some passages from her response:

Thanks for your note the other day. Must have been hard to write. I just wanted to say none of this was your fault. You were out there doing what you love. Staying true to yourself always. Could have happened to anyone. You have nothing to apologize for. You are amazing and so strong. Always joking around and being positive. Your rate of healing is incredible.

I am so thankful that you didn't give up out there. You don't think you are a hero, but you are. You saved me too because I can't live without you... Also Abby needs a dad. Who is going to scare away all her boyfriends?

Yes, this is hard on me too. I am stressed and I try not to show it. I kind of fail at that. I will survive though and always be there for you.

I know you are going through a lot. My heart breaks for you. No one should ever have to endure what you did. It is not fair. I won't pretend to understand only be there for you.

Just know you are doing great. I am so proud of you. Keep healing and kicking ass... I love you so much and I promise to show you every day for the rest of our lives!

Over the course of his hospital stay, Jeremy had a steady stream of family and friends dropping by, including outfitter Jim Turner and the "ladies" from the Lodge at Panther River, Amanda and Jay, and Ryden, Amanda's son. Their first visit, at Jeremy's request, was seven days after the incident. "Jay was really excited to see him," recalls Amanda. 'We were surprised how good he looked. Jay was blown away." Added Ryden: "He just looked so different. He was put back together."

They brought a hand-drawn card which read: "Thank you for fighting. Thank you for showing us how incredible a human being can be. Your strength. Your determination. Your heart. It was the most beautiful thing we have ever witnessed in our lives!"

Jeremy would often seek advice from his visitors about how he could be successful during his next bighorn sheep hunt. One day, after a visit by Amanda, Jeremy told his wife he was anxious to go sheep hunting, most likely with Amanda as his guide. Joyce, a very calm and collected woman, lost it, fearful again for her husband's life. She went for a walk to calm down. And she did. Over time she would come to better acknowledge her husband's passion for the outdoors and, with certain strong safety precautions in place, allow it to resume.

Nathan Sieppert, whom he had known since high school, and Jeremy's older friend Wayne Brennen were frequent visitors. On day one, Wayne, a friend for 15 years, and Joyce had established a password that allowed people to visit Jeremy. If you didn't know it, or were asking too many questions, security would escort you out. Which occurred regularly at the start. Boundaries and privacy were integral to maintain focus on healing for the entire family.

Early in Jeremy's hospital stay, Joyce and Wayne established a protocol to help him with his nightmares. Joyce had been stroking Jeremy's foot, one of the areas of his body that had never been subject to the bear attack. Touching it never startled or triggered him. While softly rubbing his foot, Joyce reassured Jeremy that he was safe now.

September 8 was a huge day for Jeremy. It was the day he looked in the mirror for the first time without his head fully wrapped in bandages. Dr. Friesen, the psychologist, had been working closely with him to help him through the nightmares and horrific flashbacks. She was seven or eight months pregnant with her first child, and she came to see Jeremy for chats every afternoon she worked.

Dr. Friesen has worked with many trauma and burn victims, including policemen, nurses and ambulance drivers. After trauma, she says, it is the incident that holds all the power, not the victim. Jeremy's nightmares were partially driven by recalling the sound of his bones crunching as the grizzly munched on his face. Some people try to avoid thinking about the trauma they endured instead of confronting it. That avoidance gives the incident so much more power. Others embellish the incident's magnitude and cascade into depression. Dr. Friesen recalls a person who suffered a small thumb injury but was afraid to use his arm for a full month.

Not Jeremy. Not his style. Not in his DNA. He was

hell-bent on recovery, working constantly to hone a sharp sense of humour to aid in the healing. Joyce says the humour development really took off when he was in hospital. It was important for Jeremy to process the mauling and realize he was a survivor, not a victim. Dr. Friesen recalls Jeremy became particularly good at expressing himself and talking about the attack. "It is truly an inspirational story," she says.

Along with Joyce, she had helped prepare Jeremy for the unveiling of his face in front of the mirror for the first time. "I kept saying, 'You are going to be pleasantly surprised,' over and over again," the psychologist remembers, crediting the surgeons for their exceptional work putting Jeremy's face back together. She thought it was likely to take several sessions before Jeremy moved from far back in the hospital room to stand directly in front of the mirror.

It was a tense, scary moment as he prepared to see his own image. He had no idea what to brace for. Dr. Friesen says he started about four metres back and within minutes had moved forward to stand immediately in front of the mirror. "Once he was on a roll, he was on a roll," she says.

"I saw what I looked like, and it wasn't as bad as I had worried it might be," remembers Jeremy. "I wasn't as shocked as I thought I would be. Most of the swelling was down. The scars between my eyes were gone. I looked pretty good."

Adds Dr. Friesen: "He really did look fantastic for what he had gone through." She was one of the first recipients of a gift from Jeremy of an inscribed Badlands baseball cap which read, humorously, "Lindsay, we had some grizzly tales together." It was signed "The Grizzly Dude."

Dr. Friesen, Jeremy recalls, left the unit very soon after that momentous day, and he was assigned a new psychologist. Once again, Jeremy talked about the mauling and his miraculous escape that had ended up with him in the hospital room. When the new psychologist said, "I don't believe you," Joyce lost it. She angrily ordered the psychologist out of the room. And then Joyce, remembers Jeremy, went to the nursing station and told the charge nurse: "If that psychologist ever comes back, I will kick her out of room myself."

Adds Dr. Friesen: "Myself, I had no doubt his story was true. You could not make it up if you tried."

On September 12, still seriously worried about both blurred and double vision, Jeremy was taken to Rockyview Hospital to see famed eye doctor Dr. Howard Gimbel. During a career spanning four decades, Dr. Gimbel has received dozens of awards and distinctions. But his greatest satisfaction, he says, comes from restoring or improving the vision of his patients. "Helping individual patients and teaching other doctors so they can help their own patients are the greatest satisfaction and honour I can imagine for any ophthalmologist," says Dr. Gimbel, an industry innovator born into a pioneering farm family in southern Alberta. The doctor, says Jeremy, was amazing.

According to Jeremy, Dr. Gimbel remains astonished that the eye damage from the mauling wasn't more permanent or of greater significance. Jeremy was told he needed to retrain the eye that was damaged during the mauling. The best way to do so, the doctor recommended, would be to focus intently on the movement of people. When he was later allowed to take short visits away from the Foothills Medical Centre, Jeremy and Joyce would head to the mall. They didn't go to purchase anything, just to watch people moving around. In doing so, Jeremy was retraining his eye. And it worked. At the time of his first meeting with Dr. Gimbel, his eyesight was 20/30 with lens correction. Today it is 20/25, which is slightly below average.

September 28 was another momentous day for Jeremy. It was less than a week after the failed operation, and his skull remained heavily bandaged. A nurse asked how he was feeling. And he replied, "Fantastic." In return, Jeremy was given his first day pass to leave the hospital grounds. He felt overjoyed, much like a high school student provided with a hall pass.

His head wrapped in what Jeremy said looked like a turban with draining tubes hanging out, he was picked up by Wayne Brennen and Nathan Sieppert. They brought Jeremy's rifle with them, and all three headed off to the Shooting Edge, Calgary's largest indoor shooting range and the only one with a 50-yard indoor rifle range. Jeremy had fretted that with his frail hands and limited eyesight, he would be unable to even hold a gun, let alone fire it with any accuracy.

Given his appearance, range staff asked whether he was healthy enough to shoot, or even had the strength to fire his weapon. Jeremy, of course, said most certainly, even though "I was unsure I could hold a gun." When his bullets hit the target, Jeremy was elated. He took that target back to the hospital and showed his new prize possession to the nurses. Within 15 minutes, Dr. Nickerson was in his hospital room, asking about how the day went. He seemed pleased that Jeremy was again doing what he had been so passionate about before the mauling.

Jeremy has other fond memories of the time spent in hospital, some funny but most reflecting the tremendous care he received from compassionate staff. He remembers two orderlies talking within earshot once, when he was being moved from intensive care to the burn unit. One asked the other: "Did you hear about the big fight last night?" The other replied, "No." The first was quick to explain: "It was Jeremy against the grizzly, and I think Jeremy won."

Every morning at five a.m. he had a date with Cindy, a nurse who cleaned the "gunk out of my eyes." Other nurses helped him sit up so they could put water on his back when he felt it was on fire.

On the day of his release, a Badlands representative

from Manitoba dropped off caps, cups and other memorabilia. Jeremy had been a pro-staffer for the company, which bills itself as making the best hunting apparel, packs and accessories on the planet; Jeremy's main task had been to test equipment. Jeremy signed many caps and gave those and other mementos to the hospital staff who had treated him with such kindness.

"I was happy. I was excited. I was ready to go home," says the outdoorsman who many experts believe should have died in the woods 36 days earlier.

The next day, Jeremy wanted to go back to the Lodge at Panther River to see Amanda, Ryden and Jay. Most importantly he wanted to return to the gate at the entrance to the trail to the North Burnt Timber drainage. At the gate, overcome with emotion, he burst into tears.

On the drive back to the lodge, Joyce and Jeremy spotted a couple of spruce grouse. They got out, grabbed their shotguns from the back of the truck, and trailed the birds. Each took one, and they fired at the same time.

CHAPTER 13

Alberta Fish and Wildlife Bear Experts' Investigation

August 24, 2017

Alberta Fish and Wildlife began its extensive investigation just after four p.m. on August 24, when Sundre district officer Adam Mirus received a call that a person horrifically mauled by a bear was en route by private helicopter to the Sundre Hospital.

After contacting the unit duty inspector, Mirus was directed to immediately go to the hospital to meet the survivor and begin collecting evidence. Todd Ponich, the regional problem-wildlife specialist, was quickly contacted at his home about two hours' drive away, in Stettler. The decision was made that the 24-year veteran would leave for Sundre and begin co-ordinating the investigation as well as efforts to trap and euthanize the bear.

Ponich is a recognized North American expert in bear behaviour, especially human/wildlife conflict. He entered the field in 1984, when Alberta determined it needed to develop expertise after a fatal mauling in Waterton National Park. He has taught wildlife officers and first responders across multiple states and Canadian provinces, and he tells you proudly, "I love everything about bears."

Paul Weisser, who would act as the predator response team lead, was the next to be called in. Paul had grown up watching his dad, also a Fish and Wildlife officer, who had served as an early predator response team member. That sparked a keen interest in knowing everything possible about grizzlies, which Paul encountered several times while guiding in the Yukon and Northwest Territories before becoming an officer himself.

At the hospital, Officer Mirus told his superiors that the survivor had severe head, face, neck and calf injuries. The survivor could not speak, the officer said, and therefore Jeremy communicated with him mostly via hand signals only. He recounted the information he'd received from Jeremy about the attack, and told them he had been able to secure some clothing for laboratory analysis from the survivor prior to his transport to Foothills Medical Centre in Calgary. These initial items included orange pants with a puncture mark near the right pocket, blue-and-yellow boxer shorts, a purple undershirt, an outer shirt, hiking boots and a phone.

Asked if he had been hunting, Jeremy had nodded yes. He was asked where the mauling took place, and the area was narrowed down to the Burnt Timber drainage. At one point Jeremy was able to say, "Coordinates on phone." Upon analysis of the phone, two coordinates for hunting camps were found.

It would take hours and hours of difficult searching in scorching heat before officers would find the site of the actual mauling. Jeremy had only been on his way to the planned campsite when he was attacked, not at it. That night at the district warehouse, the exhibits from Jeremy were catalogued and prepared for transport to the special investigations and forensic services laboratory in Edmonton. At the same time, steps were taken to build a team to go into the site the next morning. In total, eight different officers put 333 hours into the investigation and trapping efforts.

The remote site was accessible only via helicopter. Due to the extreme fire hazard at the time and the current forest fire situations in Alberta and Banff National Park, fire patrols were being conducted daily. Weather conditions were extreme, with tough, smoky conditions and temperatures peaking in the mid-30s.

Officers believed the attack site was at the top end of the basin bordered by Banff National Park and Don Getty Provincial Park. In 2014, another grizzly bear incident had occurred in the same drainage. Although there were no injuries, the hunter was tormented by a grizzly. He was able to escape. The area was closed as a precaution, and the bear was not pursued.

August 25, 2017

The day after the attack, as Jeremy's first major surgery neared completion, officers met for a briefing at the Sundre office. The clothing exhibits were given to officer William Rasmussen for transport to Edmonton. Arrangements had been made through Alberta Agriculture and Forestry to use a helicopter to access the remote location. The plan was that the helicopter would meet officers at the Red Deer ranger station and then transport the team in from there. At the ranger station, officers received a helicopter safety briefing, and the pilot was provided a bear briefing by Officer Ponich, the problem-wildlife expert. Due to helicopter size restrictions, Ponich, Weisser and district officer Kyle Lester went into the site first. The helicopter then returned for the additional officers.

The goal on the ground was for Ponich, Weisser and Lester to attempt to locate the camp as well as the possible attack site. They were dropped off at the head of the basin and immediately saw grizzly diggings. Their gear was left at drop-off and would remain there until the campsite was located.

After an extensive search, the officers believed no campsite existed nearby. Nor did they find any evidence of the attack or the survivor's belongings. The search was expanded down the drainage. Other officers were asked to conduct aerial helicopter searches of the sides of the drainage. The second campsite that had been identified by GPS was likely a satellite camp, and the officers believed Jeremy had not established it before the attack.

The search continued down the drainage for hours. The officers knew Jeremy had been riding a bicycle, and the terrain they were searching was certainly not conducive to that type of travel. They encountered several waterfalls along the bottom of the drainage. There were very steep side walls. The best way to travel was in the creek bottom. The aerial helicopter search had not located any sign of Jeremy's belongings. It was truly tough slogging in the intense heat and smoke-filled air.

About halfway down the drainage, on the south side, officers found a horse trail. This was likely the best direction for them to follow as it was suitable for travel by bike.

Meanwhile, officers Paul Sywanyk and Phil Marasco went to the outfitters' camp that they knew Jeremy had passed through on his way out. There, they discovered several empty shell casings, and they found blood on chairs, on tent poles and on the tent itself. Inside the tent, they found the ransacked cupboard along with the food and empty juice boxes Jeremy had taken from it.

At approximately six p.m., more than seven hours after the search began, Jeremy's bike was located along the trail, almost four kilometres from the initial drop-off site, down incredibly challenging steep terrain. It was in a weird position, up a tree as if someone had tossed it there. Approximately five metres past the bike, they found Jeremy's backpack, open, its contents spread out. Several spent rifle shells lay nearby. Berry-filled bear scat was also found around the backpack in several locations. This was a prime haven for bears and their cubs to feast on berries.

The helicopter pilot was notified of the find. The area was not accessible for landing, but officers determined another location 200 metres downstream where gear could be tossed out to the ground. Using handsaws dropped from the helicopter, they were then able to widen a clearing for the helicopter to land. Ponich disembarked and photographed all visible belongings.

It was getting late; finding the site had taken far longer than expected. It would take several trips to get everyone back to the Red Deer ranger station. The belongings were removed to the warehouse for further processing. Visible grizzly bear hairs found on the pack were collected. The bicycle was left on scene because of limited space on the helicopter. It would be collected later.

About the same time, the hunters Jeremy had tried to attract by firing his rifle contacted Mirus, the duty officer in Sundre. They told him they had seen Jeremy earlier that day, riding his bicycle past them on the trail. Shortly after that, they heard what sounded like more than 40 gunshots. They did not think anything of it at the time.

That night, Ponich drove to Jeremy's vehicle, still

parked at the Lodge at Panther River. He found large quantities of blood, but there was no trace of bear evidence that might have fallen from the victim. He then returned to the Sundre district office, where the exhibits brought from the mauling site were secured for forensic testing. At 30 minutes past midnight, he filed an update report to his superiors. It had been a long day.

August 26, 2017

Another busy day started with a briefing at the Sundre district office as the team readied to trap the grizzly that had attacked Jeremy. The exhibits taken from the scene were catalogued and prepared for transport to the Edmonton laboratory. These included Jeremy's binoculars and case, with dried blood and animal hairs in it. Ponich advised Dr. Richard Jobin, the forensic unit manager, that more exhibits would soon be coming to him for analysis. Ponich spoke to Joyce and asked permission to retrieve the attack selfie from Jeremy's phone. She gave permission on the condition the photograph would not be given out or used except by the wildlife specialist in reporting the mauling.

He then met with friends of the survivor, including Nathan and Jack Sieppert as well as Wayne Brennen, who had already spent several hours with Jeremy after his initial surgeries. They were in the Sundre area to retrieve Jeremy's vehicle and cellphone.

With much to accomplish at the attack site, Ponich decided another officer should be the first to interview

Jeremy at Foothills Medical Centre. He prepared questions for officer John Tetz, who was based much closer to the hospital, to ask Jeremy that afternoon.

Ponich was taken by helicopter to the attack site, where Weisser and his predator response team were already hard at work. The forestry department had also provided a crew to further clear the landing area. A family culvert trap — a tube large enough to fit a bear and cub inside — had been slung into the site. When a bear grabs the bait inside, the door behind slams shut, trapping the animal. In addition, snare-based traps — two cubbies and one trail set — were established.

Ponich landed beside one of the already built cubbies. Weisser had examined the bicycle and removed several grizzly bear hairs from the sprocket area on the back wheel. With the traps completed, Weisser and his team left. When the helicopter returned, Ponich and another problem-wildlife specialist loaded Jeremy's bicycle and returned to Sundre. He then spoke to Officer Tetz regarding his interview with Jeremy and Joyce. Jeremy had asked whether anyone had found his hat and glasses.

Office Tetz summarized Jeremy's account of the attack, including his belief that he had grabbed the bear's testicles. Given the differences between defensive and predatory attack styles, Tetz believed this attack to have more predatory behaviours associated with it. A predatory attack by a grizzly is rare: it means the bear is coming directly after you with intent to harm. Playing dead won't work.

Ponich received forensic information based on DNA analysis from Dr. Jobin confirming the attack was by a grizzly. More analysis was to take place. The sex of the animal was yet to be determined.

Ponich, Weisser and one other officer were flown to the site. They found no evidence of bear activity and no footage of bear activity on the trail camera they had installed. They freshened bait trails in the area and used information from Joyce to search for Jeremy's glasses and baseball cap. The cap was found at the base of a small tree that officers believed to be the one Jeremy had tried to climb when fleeing the angry grizzly. The tree was extremely small — approximately three to four metres high and maybe seven centimetres in diameter. With the area under an extreme fire hazard warning, the officers returned to the ranger station. The temperature exceeded 30 degrees Celsius, and it was an extremely smoky day. The helicopter would conduct patrols.

Later that day they went in again to check the traps and look for Jeremy's glasses. The glasses were not found, nor was there any bear activity.

The area had already been marked with signage. With mapping personnel returning to the site the next day, a map of the off-limits area, which had been started at the Turner outfitters' camp, was now prepared for social media use.

August 28, 2017

Ponich spoke with Dr. Jobin. The full DNA analysis showed that the attack was by a female grizzly bear. Given Jeremy's statement that he had grabbed the bear's testicles, Ponich asked the forensic scientist how confident he was of the findings. Dr. Jobin's confidence was extremely high.

Ponich also arranged for the return of Jeremy's Tikka T3 300 Win Mag rifle with Quigley scope, his Specialized Rockhopper mountain bike, his bike helmet and his Badlands baseball cap. They would be delivered to Joyce by officer Kyle Lester the next day.

Two helicopter patrols were conducted into the attack site, one at 11 a.m. and the other at 6:30 p.m. No activity had been captured on camera, and no bear had been caught. The bait was freshened. Officers did see an animal in the trees directly in front of the helicopter, but it turned out to be a mule deer, not a grizzly bear.

They also went to the outfitters' camp to examine the area for evidence of bear activity. There were no signs that grizzlies had been there. They posted temporary closure signs at the camp and the trailhead leading into the valley.

August 29, 2017

After updating Joyce, Ponich met with the team and again went to the ranger station to board the helicopter. The trapping site was checked, and yet again nothing was found. On the afternoon trip, the pilot reported that three grizzly bears were seen in the drainage during fire patrols. One bear, spotted on the north side of the drainage in a grassy area, retreated north when the helicopter approached. A sow and single cub were also seen in the creek bottom, about 125 metres from the capture site. They retreated south onto a trail that leads into Don Getty Park. At the attack site, bait was again freshened, the snares and traps inspected, and again nothing was found. Officers flew around the area to identify where the grizzlies had been observed. They did not see any bears. The temperature was still more than 30 degrees Celsius, and it was very, very smoky. Officer Lester returned home, later confirming meeting with Joyce and returning Jeremy's items. He told Ponich it had been an emotional meeting.

August 30, 2017

With the assistance of officer Matt Michaud, a second family culvert trap was taken to the ranger station to be flown into the attack site. The other traps and cameras were checked, but there had been no activity. The second family trap was slung into site and set up. Both of these traps were connected to each other and placed in a location that would not impede the helicopter, although the landing area had become tighter. Bait trails leading to the traps were refreshed. The work was carried out in scorching weather, with visibility drastically reduced due to smoke. Agriculture and Forestry continued their support, taking officers in twice daily. The helicopter conducted fire patrols in between these tasks.

August 31, 2017

Only one patrol into the site was conducted. New bait trails were set and the traps and cameras again checked, but nothing was there.

September 1, 2017

After seven fruitless days of intense effort, Fish and Wildlife officers on the ground were advised to terminate control efforts. The hunt for Jeremy's attacker was over.

After flying into the site, officers began dismantling the two family traps. The first family trap was removed, and bait from the cubbies was placed in the second culvert trap before it too was flown out. When the helicopter returned, all gear was removed and the personnel flown out for the last time until a year later, when they would return with Jeremy and Joyce. Closure signs remained at the trailhead and the outfitter camp. Due to the residual smells from the bait, Ponich recommended the area remain closed until September 15.

September 15, 2017

The closure was lifted.

February 6, 2018

As he prepared his final report, Ponich arranged to interview Jeremy, who told him he was seeing a PTSD (post-traumatic stress disorder) therapist and receiving counselling for his flashbacks, which had been occurring regularly. Jeremy asked to see the attack selfie that had been taken from his phone. Neither he nor Joyce had ever seen it. He asked for and was given a copy.

As he recounted the attack to Ponich, this time Jeremy was able to recall seeing a second bear just prior to the attack. (It is common for memory to be affected by traumatic events). The specifics of the attack remained the same. Jeremy could not explain why it wasn't until now that he remembered these details, but attending counselling was helping him understand the flashbacks that plagued him day and night

In his report, Ponich concluded:

> The area where the mauling occurred was a remote location not accessible by motor vehicle. The weather at the time of the attack was temperatures of +30° C and extremely smoky with strong winds in the drainage that persisted throughout Jeremy's efforts to save himself. The survivor had originally ridden a bicycle into the area and left by foot after the mauling. Much of the distance covered was by crawling and Jeremy fell many times.
>
> Officers attending searched an area from the top of the basin to the attack site. Approximately

three to four kilometres were covered. Signs of bears were visible at the top of the basin. These consisted of diggings that were old and likely from the spring.

No other sign of bear activity was seen until the officers approached the attack scene. The attack scene was the first area that contained ripe buffalo berries. The scat found at the attack was loose, red, and consistent with a bear feeding on berries. The description of the attack was pieced together over several conversations. The original belief was the attack showed signs of predation as the survivor had been in the area for a period of time, the bear was quiet in his approach and consistent with predatory attacks, the survivor fought back and was able to defend himself. This is a consistent message provided to the public in this type of conflict.

The survivor was adamant that the bear was male but DNA analysis at the forensic lab confirmed the offending bear was a grizzly bear and a female. New information learned from the survivor now indicated the existence of a second bear. Tracks were never found at the site and DNA analysis only produced one profile. This is not limiting in the decision or the classification as it is common that a sow defends her young and the young are never involved.

The ground at the location was extremely hard and no tracks were ever found. The presence of the second bear and then the quick attack by the sow is consistent defensive behaviour, although the actions of the survivor to fight back is not the recommended response. This may be a reason for separate attacks occurring. The break in the attacks could have been as a result of the survivor's action in placing his hand in the mouth and grabbing what he believed were testicles. The survivor stated that the bear's reaction was to vomit and make loud noises. Once the bear released and recovered, she then realized the threat continued to exist and resumed her attack. Given the information of the survivor that two bears were present and that the cub passed in front of him moments before the attack; given the DNA analysis that the offending bear was female; given the physical sighting of a sow with a single cub within 200 yards of the attack site, I believe that although the actions of the survivor were not the recommended reaction, the attack was a grizzly bear sow defending her offspring.

I suggest the classification of the attack as defensive.

To this day, Jeremy is glad the grizzly that mauled him was not trapped and euthanized. "She was just a mother, doing what mothers do," he says. "She was protecting her young. You can't blame her for that."

And Ponich, who has investigated more than 20 attacks, mainly by grizzly bears, remains in awe that

Jeremy survived, given the extent of his injuries and the remote location. "There are so many elements of the attack that could have caused his death, including bleeding out," he says. "My takeaway from Jeremy is the incredible desire a human has to survive. Most incidents don't end well. It is a remarkable story."

CHAPTER 14

The Return to Hunting

BEING OUTDOORS IS SECOND NATURE TO JEREMY AND has been since he started fishing as a toddler and shot his first deer at age 7. He rarely consumes alcohol, recalling that, growing up, a case of beer cost about the same as a tank of gas to go fishing. To him, money spent fishing provided better value and much more fun.

Jeremy also thrives on disciplined structure and keeping busy. With ADHD, he just can't sit around doing nothing. As Joyce attests, that takes a toll on everyone. After being discharged from hospital and before going back to work, he was going stir-crazy hanging around at home. He yearned to return to the outdoors — hunting and fishing and, of course, work. Also top of mind was that, in hospital, he had been lucky enough to win, in a draw he had entered before the attack, a tag to hunt a famed mule deer buck, a big-game animal for which Alberta is internationally renowned.

Some of his first visitors at the hospital had been the owners of Harmony Beef, of Rocky View County, just outside Calgary. Even though fresh from major surgery, he told them what parts needed to be ordered for a project he was undertaking as their plant electrician. They brought a card with the phrase Tough Cookie (spelled tuhf kook-e) and a photograph of a delicious-looking chocolate chip cookie. Nailing the attributes that make Jeremy unique, it read:

- Someone with just the right mix of sweetness and strength.
- One who doesn't crumble under pressure.
- A fighter who is too busy kicking butt to sit down and cry, but knows it is okay to do both.
- A person who doesn't always ask for support but has lots of friends who would do anything to help.

Jeremy remained nervous he would be unable to ever again showcase his outdoorsmanship, which had been so impressive before the mauling occurred. He had little strength, no feeling in several areas of his body; he could not close his eyelids, was unable to regulate his body temperature and had poor eyesight. Any one of these setbacks could be devastating to a hunter. The outing to the shooting range, however, had built his confidence. He knew that maybe the greatest obstacle to returning to hunting was Joyce, the woman he so dearly loved.

In hindsight, Jeremy shouldn't have worried so much. Joyce is an extraordinarily strong woman who will readily tell you she is not the type of wife to demand that her husband give up the parts of his life that he is passionate about. "Not really that kind of wife," says Joyce.

But not being that kind of wife didn't mean she was going to roll over submissively and play dead either. There were new rules to be negotiated, new procedures to follow, and new equipment to purchase, some of it over time. To start, there would be no more hunting alone in forests where bears are found. Riding alone deep into a dense forest on a mountain bike would never occur again. Joyce would always prefer Jeremy hunt with one other person minimum, even on prairie landscapes where grizzly bears are seldom if ever seen.

Over time, Joyce would become more comfortable with Jeremy hunting alone again in lower-risk areas. The prairies, with their wide-open spaces, would always be her preference over heavily treed forests. Bear bangers, which make an extremely loud noise and release flares 40 metres into the air, would now be *de rigueur*, with Jeremy consistently strapping them to his binocular case. And so would bear spray in an easily reached holster strapped to his chest. Jeremy and Joyce would also purchase a Garmin inReach satellite communicator. The rugged device uses 100 per cent global Iridium satellite coverage to permit two-way messaging anywhere in the world. In case of emergency, the interactive SOS allows a person to communicate back and forth and receive confirmation that help is on the way. Joyce expected regular check-in messages from Jeremy ensuring his safety and noting his location.

They had a beautiful red-haired daughter to care about too. No more fumbling around with a small first aid kit like the one in his backpack when the grizzly attacked. Jeremy purchased an Elite First Aid Tactical Trauma Kit #3, just one step below what ambulance personnel carry. Never again would he be caught short. The kit is preferred by professionals, including medics, first responders, paramedics, combat lifesavers and army personnel. "You could probably do surgery with what is in that kit," he says, noting it contains sutures and devices to close wounds, in addition to scalpels.

Only a couple of days after leaving the hospital, Jeremy went for the weekend to again meet his friend Don Logan, who was camping with his family at Crimson Lake Provincial Park. The nearby area features wide-open fields and lightly treed spaces. It is more like farmland than the type of terrain where bears hang out. It was the perfect place for Don to shoot his first-ever whitetail deer.

"He knows this great field," remembers Don, noting Jeremy was still recovering from leg surgery and unable to walk quickly. He even brought a chair with him. "At the edge of the woods, he hits the deck. There's a deer in the field over the hill."

He remembers Jeremy slowly standing as he waited for the deer to come over the hill. Jeremy was concerned his eyesight was too poor to take solid aim. He did not have sufficient arm strength to lift his rifle to shoot from a standing position. He had to rest the weapon in the crook of a tree as he followed the deer.

Don was just happy to be learning more about the outdoors with Jeremy as his expert guide. "The plan was for me to shoot my first deer," he recalls. "He got so excited and asked if I would mind if he took the shot. I told him no problem."

Jeremy told Don to take the second shot if he missed. There would be no need. When the animal appeared, Jeremy fired, felling the deer immediately with a single shot. He knew then that he still had some skills. After loading the deer in the truck, Jeremy dropped Don off at the campsite. He spent the night in his truck.

It was only a few weeks later, in late November, that Don and Jeremy had an unforgettable experience on a blustery freezing day hunting on a Hutterite colony in southern Alberta. Jeremy was wanting to fill his mule deer buck tag while Don was still seeking his whitetail deer.

Jeremy and Don were met by Martin Hofer as they drove into the yard of the Jenner Hutterite Colony, about 250 kilometres southeast of Calgary, on a snowy day with temperatures around minus 20 degrees Celsius. The colony has about 100 members.

Often compared to Amish or Mennonites, Hutterites are a communal people belonging to a peace-oriented Anabaptist sect. The 2016 census recorded 370 Hutterite colonies in Canada, with the majority located in Alberta speaking both English and German. Faith, family and labour-intensive hard work are core to their way of life.

The Jenner Hutterites allow hunting on their large property, which is filled with magnificent geographical features, especially large coulees in the Alberta badlands. Coulees are generally gullies or ravines, often dry ones, which have been sculpted over the centuries by the action of moving water. These landscapes, the product of intense erosion by water over time, are excellent places for animals to hide from howling winds and seek protection from predators and hunters.

Hofer, then 31 and working in the communal dairy, exchanged cellphone numbers with Don. It was not his normal practice, but that day it would result in likely saving the lives of the two hunters. To this day, Hofer has no idea why he decided to take Don's number and give him his. Maybe, he thinks, it was because of the cold and the heavy snow that was falling that late-November day. Or that both Don and Jeremy had fortuitously driven their own trucks, providing a chance to chat while one parked.

It was, however, normal practice to have hunters stay on the rudimentary roads that criss-cross the large property and not venture off them or into the coulees. Staying on the so-called wild roads was much safer.

Jeremy was driving his truck down one of the back roads in what Don calls "whiteout conditions" when they spotted a whitetail deer in the distance ahead.

Jeremy jumped on the accelerator to catch up, only to plow into a large snowbank and slip off the road. The truck lifted off the road and stuck in the muddy area and growing snowdrift.

For the next two hours, they tried in vain to get the truck unstuck. Jeremy was still unable to normally regulate his body temperature. He was absolutely freezing despite keeping the truck always running and the heater blasting. Their efforts were fruitless, and it keep getting colder, with Jeremy near hypothermia.

Don decided to try to call Hofer, who was back at the colony, between 15 and 20 minutes away. But there was no cell service. He had to walk about a kilometre in the snow before he got a signal. Hofer was getting ready for the evening church service when the SOS call came in around 6:30 p.m. from Don's wife. She had been the only person with whom Don could connect.

Hofer and Don then connected by cell. The looming challenge was to tell Hofer where to find him. Not an easy task in huge coulee-filled fields in a blinding snowstorm. Jeremy and Don looked around, and it appeared they were between two large mounds that looked like large boobs. Don also texted a map of his location.

"Oh, you are in boobland," said Hofer, the dairyman. "I know where you are, and I will be there soon."

Finding them took longer than hoped. Don and Jeremy could see Hofer's truck going up and down makeshift roads but not near the coulee where they were stuck inside. They began setting off bear bangers, with their loud noise and intense flares. "If Jeremy had not brought bear bangers, I think we would still be out there," says Don. A few minutes later, the Hutterite arrived.

"They were in the middle of nowhere," recalls Hofer. "They were way off the road. I should have been giving them crap. How can you give someone crap when they are almost freezing to death?"

In darkness, Hofer used his truck to pull the two hunters to level ground and then drove ahead about a kilometre up the "wild road" and waited there so that he could lead them back to the yard and his home to warm up. When they failed to show, he went back, only to find the transmission undercarriage and crankshaft of Jeremy's truck in pieces. After being kept running for more than two hours while submerged in the snowbank, it had become a block of ice. When Jeremy pressed on the accelerator, it came apart, spewing transmission oil. Don says it also caught fire, forcing the two to jump out. An hour or so later, the truck had been towed back to the yard.

"The wife made them a nice warm supper," said Hofer, noting that Jeremy especially needed to get warm — and very, very quickly. The homemade raspberry wine helped.

During supper, Jeremy told Hofer and his German-speaking children about his battle with the grizzly bear in the Burnt Timber less than three months earlier. He talked about the importance of setting achievable, near-term goals. Hofer asked if he could invite his brother over. Within a short while, Don says, he thinks about half the men in the colony had gathered to listen to Jeremy. They were enthralled. "I will always remember the look on the faces of the children when Jeremy took his cap off," remembers Don. Jeremy's heavily damaged scalp was still healing.

"When we think grizzly bear, we think dead," Hofer says, still amazed Jeremy survived.

Later that night, Don drove Jeremy home in his truck. It was yet another day Don will ever forget.

A week later, Jeremy was back in the same colony, practically in the same location, as he sought the mule deer buck for which he had been awarded the hunting tag. This time he was in a rented truck because his was still under repair.

That Friday, he spotted a mule deer entering a large coulee and heading down into the trees. He watched for hours on the edge of the ravine, hoping the deer would surface or at least become visible. When darkness fell, he left empty-handed, vowing to be back early the next morning.

Alberta's mule deer are among the heaviest found anywhere, often surpassing 140 kilograms, and they have impressive antlers noted for their exceptional height, incredible mass and dark coloration. The southern Alberta prairie zones, where Jeremy was hunting, consist primarily of rolling hills with rivers, deep coulees and mixed farmland. This does not mean that these deer are always out in the open and easy to find. They excel at blending into the landscape when predators are nearby. Their populations are abundant in Alberta's southern and eastern regions, and they number about 133,000 total across the province.

An hour and half before dawn the next morning, Jeremy parked his rented truck for the 3.5-kilometre trek to the edge of the coulee where he had seen the buck. With the wind blowing the wrong way, it would be a much longer, more tiring hike than planned. Jeremy skirted the coulee, walking an additional five or six kilometres to get around to the other side. As he lay on the ridge to look below, he could tell that the deer, by their fidgeting, knew something was up. He spotted a mule deer buck 700 to 730 metres away in the gully. Still unable to hold his rifle in a raised position, Jeremy had fashioned a small tripod.

He waited patiently. Over time, the buck moved closer. When the animal closed to between 400 and 450 metres, Jeremy shot. It would have been an ace shot for a trained marksman, let alone a person recovering from a mauling with bad eyesight. In case he had missed, Jeremy waited for about ten minutes before beginning his descent into the coulee. As he neared the spot where the deer would be if shot, Jeremy saw he had been successful, firing from almost half a kilometre away. The animal was dead.

After harvesting the meat and the unique antlers, he had too little strength to hoist the backpack onto his shoulders. He was still wearing a knee brace. Ultimately, he manoeuvred the loaded pack onto a very steep part of the coulee where he could lie on the backpack and shimmy into the shoulder straps. Only then could he lift it and start the long hike back to the truck, carrying everything in one load. He did not have the energy for two trips.

CHAPTER 15

One Year Later

ON AUGUST 23, 2018 — A YEAR MINUS A DAY AFTER the mauling — Jeremy returned to the Sundre area, a journey that was part healing, part filling in details about what happened, and a lot about continuing to move forward for both himself and Joyce. It was also about thanking the people who helped save him, and the officers who investigated the mauling.

The day started with a seminar for Alberta Fish and Wildlife officers and first responders taking a course both in person and via video conference about how to manage and investigate human–wildlife conflicts. It was organized by Todd Ponich, whose job responsibilities include training and certifying the elite members of the predator response team.

Jeremy remembers their stunned disbelief when he showed the attack selfie of his face and skull. After taking them through the mauling and its aftermath, Jeremy thanked the organization for the professional way they had handled the incident, start to finish. "They kept everything so quiet, and out of the media," he says, noting that no reporter or cameraperson ever came to the hospital. "The media could have been a pain in the ass."

There were only two quick bursts of coverage: once when the province released information that a mauling had taken place in the Burnt Timber drainage, and a few days later, when it was announced that a grizzly bear was responsible. Few media outlets covered the mauling. The stories were short and mostly factual. No names were released, ever.

After the training seminar, Jeremy and Joyce would make four more stops that day, the most emotional one a return to the mauling site for the first time since it occurred. Ponich and multiple-award-winning district officer John Clarke, from the Crowsnest Pass region in southern Alberta, spearheaded the return. Like Ponich, Clarke is an internationally recognized bear expert, having developed trained dogs to manage problem bears and launched leading-edge programs to protect both communities and wildlife in the bear-rich region where he is based.

Ponich and Clarke flew in first to check if any bears were visible around the attack site. It would have been horrific to have a second mauling at the exact same location, especially with wildlife officers on the scene. Although the spot remained a berry bonanza location a year later, they found no bear activity. They returned to pick up Jeremy and Joyce.

After flying in, Ponich said, Jeremy was at first unwilling to get out of the helicopter. For everyone involved, it was extremely emotional. When Jeremy finally did disembark, he appeared nervous, although there was little reason. The officers had firearms, and Ponich had told Jeremy and Joyce he was prepared to take on any bear if necessary. Both Jeremy and Joyce had bear spray strapped to the front of their chests in easily accessible shoulder holsters. Joyce's biggest concern was her husband and how adversely he might react.

Jeremy took everyone through what had happened a year earlier, showing them where his clothes had been strewn and the tree he tried to climb to escape. He pointed to the spot where 36 shell casings had been found, where he'd fired at any dark spot he could make out. He told Ponich the tree he climbed was not the small one officers had identified when his hat was found at the bottom of it. The real one was only slightly larger and would not have given him much more leverage, as a grizzly could easily climb it to yank a human out. At one point Jeremy was spooked when officer Clarke rustled the trees behind him. He immediately yelled for the officer to stop moving behind him.

A massive emotional outburst came when Jeremy walked down the steep drainage where he had tumbled more than 50 metres, crashing into the creek rocks below.

Midway down, he collapsed in tears, suffering a traumatic flashback. Ponich describes the loud sobbing as a "really good cry." Joyce prefers a "really emotional scene."

Once again, a search for Jeremy's lost glasses proved fruitless. Everyone returned to the helicopter for the flight out. For Jeremy and Joyce, the next destination was the hospital in Sundre, to thank the medical responders from the emergency department, who were surprised he would take the time to come so far and would express his thanks so genuinely and profusely. After all, they had just been doing the job for which they were trained.

At the hospital, he recalled how, as he struggled to get out of the helicopter, nurse Chantal Crawford just came behind and lifted him out with a huge bear hug to put him on the stretcher. "She is not very big," he said with a chuckle. He presented her with a baseball cap emblazoned "Chantal, the world's strongest nurse." It was signed "The Grizzly Dude."

"There are certain experiences I will never forget," she says. She knows the country around Sundre well and still feels it is almost a miracle that Jeremy survived, especially given his massive head and leg injuries as well as the deep-backcountry location where the mauling occurred. His actions, including driving an exceptionally dangerous road to the lodge, she says, took phenomenal courage. She says his "never give up attitude," propelled by an unwavering love for wife and family, is inspirational. And his exceptional knowledge of the outdoors, and his initiative in tying a sweater around his head and later using vet tape, likely saved his life, as did his knowledge that he had to keep hydrated or he would die.

Dr. Somerville, the young rural physician who had held Jeremy's head steady in the ambulance, also merited a signed hat, which read: "Dr. Jonathan — Thanks for keeping my head up." It was also signed "The Grizzly Dude."

"He was walking a hairline in terms of survival. It was impressive he was able to see where to go," said Dr. Somerville, adding he was surprised Jeremy came back, because most trauma victims don't want to return to relive a nightmarish incident.

Paramedic Jamie Orr, who had helped Jeremy breathe and kept his airways unclogged from the bleeding, also met with Jeremy and Joyce, learning more about what had taken place a year earlier and how the recovery was progressing. His hat from the Grizzly Dude was inscribed: "Jamie — Stop talking. Use your hands. Thanks for the suction."

After the hospital, they moved on to the Lodge at Panther River and a reunion with Amanda, Ryden and others who had helped save Jeremy's life. They would spend several days fishing and healing, surrounded by the spectacular nature they both love so dearly. "I just knew I wanted to go back there," says Joyce.

The first afternoon, they returned to the fence where Jeremy had burst into tears only days after his release from hospital. This time he did not cry.

The next day, Jeremy and Joyce, wearing waders and carrying bear spray, went fly-fishing for bull trout on the Panther River until Jeremy spotted sets of grizzly bear tracks on the bank. In hot waders on a warm day, they immediately decided to hike up to Dormer Lake, a spectacular, remote oasis about midway up Dormer Mountain, a 2766-metre peak easily recognizable due to its steep east face and multiple minor ridges caused by glacier scouring. Just below treeline, pristine, emerald-coloured and surrounded by dense forest, the lake is a fly-fisher's paradise fully stocked with brook trout. They had no idea who had left a rowboat there, but they used it to fish for trout considered amongst the most colourful of any trout species. It was catch-and-release, and there were plenty of fish to keep the two of them extremely happy in an area devoid of any other humans. "I was just happy to do some fishing. It was part of the healing process. It was pretty easy fishing," Joyce says.

In late afternoon they hiked back to the lodge. They had hiked 25 kilometres that day, a gruelling trek with a tough river crossing and hundreds of metres of elevation gain. In comparison, the lodge offers a guided horseback tour up to the lake that takes six hours return.

Over the next couple of days, they fished several streams in the area, but Jeremy refused to fish in the North Burnt Timber Creek, once one of their favourite places to cast one of his homemade flies. "It was probably too traumatic, I guess," surmises Joyce.

Jeremy admitted to being very nervous about hiking into the area near where the mauling occurred. "It just wasn't worth it," he recalls, noting there were lots of little willows in the area and "every time I have seen a bear, there were willows." His eyes also continue to bother him, especially in sunlight, making it difficult to see.

Dormer Lake was such a magical experience that Joyce and Jeremy decided on a whim to go camping there for a night, something they had not done even once since the mauling. They had not planned to camp when they came to the Lodge; they had not even brought any gear other than sleeping bags and Jeremy's little portable stove. Their intent had been to stay at their cabin throughout the trip. But during their hike, they spotted one of the Lodge's remote outfitters' camps near the shore and decided they wanted to stay there. Terry Safron took them up to the lake in his helicopter — Jeremy's first time in the black helicopter since the emergency flight to the hospital in Sundre.

If there is anything predictable about Joyce and Jeremy, it is that they are so unpredictable. They love to do things on the spur of the moment, acting on whims. Camping deep in the dense forest in grizzly bear territory just happened. They were both nervous but realized it was yet another way to exorcise the demons associated with the attack and speed the recovery. For added protection, they had a rifle and bear spray, and the camp was surrounded with an electrified fence. "The fence especially made me feel safer," recalls Joyce.

The next day, as they luxuriated in the peace, quiet and solitude they adore, the fly-fishing was fantastic. The journey out would be almost as easy as the helicopter ride in: Amanda and Ryden arrived at the lake on horseback with two other horses in tow. With radiant smiles, Jeremy and Joyce rode into the sunset and back to the Lodge before their journey home the next day.

Two weeks later, Jeremy and Joyce, along with his older sister, Jennifer, and her husband, Jason, would be back on the road, heading to Crowsnest Pass in southern Alberta to learn more about bears and how to use bear spray. The area is one of the most active for both black and grizzly bears in the province and, with a team of volunteers and wildlife officers, has one of the most advanced protection programs anywhere. Under the theme "keeping people safe and wildlife wild," a multi-hour training program is offered twice yearly. It fills up quickly.

Put on by the Crowsnest Pass BearSmart Association, it covers everything from diet and scat to common travel routes, with a special focus on sows with cubs and what to do during an encounter, whether predatory or defensive. Of special interest to Jeremy was how to use bear spray, using an inert substance in the can. He learned and practised how to target bears, the distance the spray shoots, the likely bear movement and how to avoid obstacles in the way.

"I learned a lot, and that some of the things I did were wrong and probably not the optimum course of action experts would have recommended when the bear attacked. It was great to learn the best techniques if ever I am confronted by a bear again, although I pray it will never happen again," he says with a chuckle. "I still use the fake bear spray and do a quick training session every time I go out into the bush with someone where there might be bears. I do it every time, even if the person with me has already had the training."

CHAPTER 16

Don and Jeremy's Ewe Adventure

SLIGHTLY MORE THAN A YEAR AFTER JEREMY HAD been released from hospital, he and Don met for yet another hunting adventure that would rival their wild time at the Hutterite colony. After four years of trying and failing to secure a special hunting licence for a non-trophy sheep, Jeremy found out in August he had finally been successful.

Alberta uses a priority point system to draw for licences, giving applicants one additional point each year they fail, thus increasing their odds for success in future draws. Jeremy thought he was probably due to be drawn in 2018, but many outdoorsmen wait much longer.

In 2018, 13,161 Alberta residents applied for a special licence to hunt a non-trophy sheep, which is any female or a male under a year old, as opposed to a mature ram with its massive, curled horns. A total of 273 lucky hunters received a licence. By 2020, the number of annual applicants had jumped to 15,213, with six fewer special licences awarded.

Jeremy knew well the terrain of Wildlife Management Unit 416, the area his permit allowed him to hunt. It starts where the eastern boundary of Banff National Park intersects the height of land between the Red Deer River drainage and the Panther River drainage. It also includes land between the Burnt Timber Creek drainage and the Red Deer River drainage back to the eastern boundary of Banff National Park and then along the park boundary.

On September 20, about an hour before daylight, Don and Jeremy parked Jeremy's truck near the Ya Ha Tinda Ranch for what was to be a four-day, three-night camping and hunting trip. The trip did not last that long. It was cut short by the freezing cold and a howling September snowstorm.

Ya Ha Tinda Ranch is the only federally operated working horse ranch in Canada. Owned and managed by Parks Canada, it has been used since 1917 to train and winter working horses used by wardens to patrol national parks, especially the mountain national parks. The name translates to "little prairie in the mountains" in the language of nearby Stoney Indigenous People. The site is a geological oddity, an oasis of prairie grassland ringed by towering mountains. Banff National Park is in the distance. Covering about 40 square kilometres and running

27 kilometres along the north bank of the Red Deer River, the ranch is home to grizzlies, wolves, cougars, moose, deer and bighorn sheep. At peak time, it has about a hundred horses. It was once home to about 3,000 elk seeking to escape predators, especially in winter. Today only a few hundred call the ranch home.

Sporting heavy packs and wearing fishing waders, Don and Jeremy crossed the Red Deer River where it was waist-deep. Don was in tremendous shape. Two weeks later, he would run a 50-kilometre ultra-marathon along outdoor trails. He had been training since January, sparked in part by the focus, determination and strength Jeremy had demonstrated.

They were armed to the teeth with safety precautions: bear bangers, bear spray, the satellite device to regularly text Joyce and friend Wayne — even an extra, more powerful rifle, Don recalls, better suited to shoot a bear than a sheep. After they hid their waders, it was time to climb, up, and up, and up. Each was carrying about 40 kilograms of gear on his back.

The plan the two had prepared was to climb the steep cliffs of Barrier Mountain to Ice Lake, which was located well above treeline, about three-quarters of the way up the peak of the 2682-metre mountain. There, they would set up camp, maybe climb up to look over the top, and hunt for sheep in the area around the lake.

They climbed for about ten hours straight the first day but never made it to the lake. As they got higher, the misty rain turned to snow, and then much heavier snow. At times it was knee-deep. At others it was almost up to their thighs as they used crampons to edge their way up the mountain. As Jeremy says, with typical understatement, "It was a little extreme." They were also slightly under-dressed for the massive storm pummelling the side of the mountain. It was cold and getting colder, but neither of these tough outdoorsmen was a whiner.

Surrounded by fog and appearing to be amid a cloud, they climbed to a windswept ridge with some bare grass and a clump of trees where they were able to pitch their tents. They later moved higher for a look. From time to time when the fog cleared, they would spot the outlines of sheep up the mountain. But more fog would quickly roll in to blind them, and when it cleared, the sheep had disap-peared. Darkness was also coming in, with an extremely cold night ahead. They regularly updated Joyce about their location and safety by satellite.

It was so cold that the next morning Jeremy had trouble getting his pants back up because they were frozen solid. When he went over to the cliff in his boxers to pee, he looked straight down a steep several-hundred-metre drop. He also was stunned to see several sheep climbing up the ridge, about 80 metres away.

Don remembers Jeremy turning to him and saying: "I am just going to shoot this sheep and then let's go home." And that is exactly what he did, standing there in his boxers.

When struck, the ewe immediately turned and leaped off the ridge. Luckily for the hunters, it landed in a clump of trees 20 or 30 metres below. The area was too steep to harvest the meat. She needed to be brought back up to where the two had camped.

Well prepared, Jeremy had climbing rope. The two geared up, and Jeremy slid down to tie the rope around the animal. It was tough work. With Jeremy pushing from below and Don pulling from above, it took two full hours to get the animal up the ridge to where the meat could be processed and loaded into their backpacks. "Dragging the sheep up the steep ridge is probably one of the scariest things I have ever done," says Don. Still unable to start a fire, they broke camp and started home.

Jeremy carried about 60 kilograms out, Don about ten kilograms more. The trip back was quicker, because for much of it, Don says, you could slide on your bum with the pack in front of you. But it still took more than ten hours to get back to the truck.

As they neared the bottom and the Red Deer River, they heard grizzly bears snapping their jaws nearby. They moved quickly to cross the waist-deep river. They did not even stop to put on their waders, crossing in their hunting pants and hiking boots. "It was scary. We walked right through the river, not stopping," remembers Don, noting the truck was quickly loaded for immediate departure.

He also remembers Jeremy telling him that he probably would not like the taste of the animal they carried down the mountain. But "it was the most delicious meat I have ever had. It tasted fantastic, not in any way like lamb and not gamey at all."

For Jeremy, the trip was yet another milestone in his recovery. "My eyes were still not working well. To be able to climb a mountain 13 months later was amazing. I love the mountains, the views, the smell.... I was pretty ecstatic, almost overwhelmed with emotion."

CHAPTER 17

Two Years Later and Beyond

ON THE SECOND ANNIVERSARY OF THE MAULING, Joyce and Jeremy were again drawn to the magic of the outdoors, camping and fishing. With kayaks strapped to the truck, they headed to the spectacular Writing-on-Stone Provincial Park and the Milk River in southern Alberta, near the border with the United States. Jeremy and Joyce had taken a few days off work while her parents looked after Abby.

The park, a UNESCO World Heritage Site, contains a remarkable concentration of Indigenous rock carvings and paintings dating back 2,000 years. It is also home to many rattlesnakes. Although Joyce is an aquatic biologist specializing in fish, she holds a soft spot in her heart for fascinating reptiles. One of her many passions is looking for rattlesnakes in the rocks and prairie grasses. As they hiked at Writing-on-Stone, she and Jeremy spotted several, always staying far enough away to avoid any danger.

The Milk River, which flows through the park, was named by Meriwether Lewis, of the famed Lewis and Clark Expedition, in 1805. Due to silt and clay particles suspended in the water, it has a colour that Lewis compared to a teaspoon of milk in a cup of tea and that Joyce calls "absolutely gorgeous."

Basking in the sunlight, she and Jeremy manoeuvred down the river on their kayaks until they found the perfect spot to drop small anchors. When fish showed no interest in their flies, they decided to find a better spot — but somehow Jeremy's anchor had gotten snagged in the rocks or on a sunken piece of wood.

For the next couple of hours, Jeremy did everything imaginable to attempt to free the small anchor. He pulled from above, from each side, from one shoreline, from the other shoreline, and standing in water over his head. Everything. And still it would not budge. Joyce urged her husband to cut the rope — the anchor wasn't expensive, and they could easily buy another. But Jeremy was hell-bent on success. When he started something, he wanted to finish the task. Finally, the anchor came free.

"That moment was very profound for me, two years to the day after he had been mauled," remembers Joyce. "I realized in that moment how and why he survived the grizzly bear attack. He just doesn't quit. He just doesn't give up."

Adds Jeremy: "I don't know why I kept going. That's just how I am, I guess. I just don't give up on things that I know I can accomplish with a little extra effort."

Despite the traumatic attack in the Burnt Timber drainage, the outdoors and all the wonders it has to offer remain central to how the family lives its life. They began taking Abby on their fishing trips when she was only four months old. Even though it would take many months before she grew strong enough to hold her small rod and reel, she always thrived playing in the mud and water.

"Our lifestyle incorporates the children. Our children are always along for the ride," says Joyce, adding that people should not have to stop doing the things they love just because they are parents. "We are very adventurous, love camping and the outdoors."

While many of their friends are schedule-oriented, Joyce and Jeremy are more spontaneous and activity-oriented. Nap time doesn't get in the way of an opportunity to enjoy nature. With a little planning, life as they adore it goes on as usual.

As a biologist, Joyce the nature nerd loves to teach Abby about nature and claims her daughter has always been a mini-scientist, a sponge ready to lap up any information. When Joyce received a birdfeeder as a birthday present, the two would spend hours identifying birds that landed for a snack in their front yard. At the age of 3, Abby could name several by sight. Among her favourites were yellow warblers.

In August 2020, Joyce was back at the hospital, this time at the Peter Lougheed in northeast Calgary, not at the Foothills trauma centre. She was pregnant and in labour with their son, Toby, who would be eight pounds at birth, compared to six pounds, 12 ounces for Abby when she was born at the same hospital.

"Jeremy seemed nervous at the hospital when I was in labour," Joyce recalls. "I could tell he just doesn't like hospitals. He had spent too much time in a hospital room."

With COVID-19 rampant in Alberta, they were unsure whether Jeremy would be allowed into the operating room to witness the birth of their first son. Happily, he was.

Although he was still having flashbacks and nightmares, Jeremy's recovery continued to progress well. He had two additional smaller operations, both designed to restore his tear ducts, which still did not function well — water kept collecting in his eye instead of draining into the nose, especially in windy situations. Another operation was performed to repair a nostril; that required part of his ear to be transplanted. Although the operations helped, Jeremy's great progress with his eyes came about through extensive exercise designed to enable closure of his eyelids.

Although, as Joyce says, the tear ducts remain problematic, a change of jobs and access to leading-edge therapy have ended the regular nightmares Jeremy consistently suffered from even three years after the mauling. He would jump up in the middle of the night, vividly recalling the grizzly munching on his face.

He was lucky to be accepted into the Accelerated Resolution Therapy, or ART, program at Foothills

Hospital; taking it privately would have been very expensive for the family. The therapy focuses on how negative images are connected to emotional and physical reactions. Participants do not even have to talk about, or relive, their traumas.

Therapists used relaxing eye movements and a technique called "voluntary memory/image replacement" to reprogram how the distressing memories and vivid images were stored in Jeremy's brain, so that they would no longer trigger the strong physical and emotional reactions causing the nightmares.

When it succeeds, voluntary memory/image replacement — still a relatively new therapy, first developed in 2008 — processes out the old negative images and memories and restores mental health by replacing them with more positive ones. The factual reality of what happened is retained, but the negative images and associated sensations are reduced. Research has found that accessing a memory makes it flexible and able to be altered.

Jeremy learned how to process his feelings, emotions and, especially the fear, differently. He took three sessions, and the result spoke for itself. "The program worked wonders," he says. "I have not had a single nightmare since my first ART session."

COVID-19 and the birth of Joyce and Jeremy's second child stymied trips for the third and fourth anniversaries of the attack but did not stop Jeremy from adding a new outdoor skill to his repertoire: he took up gardening, something he knew could and would engage the whole family. And the green thumb he developed was as stellar as his other skills in nature.

"One day he decided to build a greenhouse in the backyard, and before you knew it the greenhouse was built," says Joyce. "When he gets into something he really gets into it. He had become fascinated with growing our own food."

The first summer, he and the family grew a plethora of produce: tomatoes, lettuce, bell peppers, green beans, carrots, radishes, zucchini the size of footballs, strawberries and herbs galore. The bounty again displayed what Jeremy could accomplish when he put his mind to a task.

CHAPTER 18

Life Lessons Learned from a Grizzly Attack

THERE IS NO ONE ELSE LIKE JEREMY EVANS. HIS RESO-lute "never give up" attitude is one of a kind. Little did he know this characteristic would someday save his life. This book is a story of survival, perseverance, love, healing and what it means to overcome the ultimate adversary. Jeremy's favourite quote comes from his high school yearbook: "I cannot change the direction of the wind, but I can adjust my sails to always reach my destination" (Jimmy Dean).

His traumatic, almost unbelievable story raises an important question: What lessons can we take from his journey from near-death to a life abundant with the outdoor pursuits and cherished loved ones so crucial to his happiness? Here, in Jeremy's words, are some of the lessons he learned by surviving and recovering from the attack:

Getting counselling or psychological help is a strength, not a sign of weakness.

Someone might ask, why does a macho man like me need psychological therapy? I say you get it because it works wonders. Getting rid of the nightmares has been a wonderful godsend to me. It was brutal jerking awake so often in the middle of the night, sweating and re-hearing the sound of the Grizzly crushing my face with her bite. It wasn't until April and May of 2021, more than three years after the mauling, that I heard about the Accelerated Resolution Therapy, or ART, program at Foothills Hospital.

The therapy reprogrammed the way in which the distressing memories and vivid images were stored in my brain so that they would no longer trigger the strong physical and emotional reactions that caused the nightmares. I have not had a nightmare since.

Always be fully prepared for the unexpected.

Danger can always lurk a few metres away in the forest, whether you are enjoying an inspirational hike, fishing, hunting or even camping. On the day of the mauling, I had nonchalantly stopped to peer out with my binoculars at a viewpoint where I had scouted for sheep many times before. I thought I was fully prepared for danger. I wasn't.

I was a strong, extremely experienced, and knowledgeable outdoorsman who knew the dangers. Perhaps out of the habit of years of backcountry sorties, I had taken my safety for granted. It was a mistake that almost killed me.

As was always the case when hunting, I had bear spray, a rifle and plenty of ammunition. Yet, on the fateful morning, none were easily within reach. The bear spray was at the bottom of my backpack. Useless. And the rifle was there too, in its holster. It wasn't even loaded with the safety on. I also carried an emergency medical kit in my pack. It was of the household variety, and inadequate to be of any substantial use to dress the massive wounds I suffered from the bear's claws and teeth.

And I was alone.

Today, my preparations are much different. I have a shoulder holster that keeps the bear spray snug against my chest, always within easy reach. Joyce has one too. I carry on me bear bangers that create the loud noise that will quickly scare predators away. I have a satellite device for texting anywhere in world. My medical kit is an emergency-grade one, and I never hunt alone in areas where bears might be present.

Human determination can defy the greatest of odds.

The experts, from doctors to veteran wildlife officers, remain astounded that I survived the horrific attack, especially given its location so distant from other humans, and the full extent of my injuries, especially to the leg, face and scalp. When you think you can't go on, rest assured you can. You have to reach deep and never give up.

There were so many times I could easily, and willingly, have given up: when I attempted to kill myself immediately after the attack, when I cascaded down the steep drainage embankment to crash against the boulders, when I couldn't find help or a satellite phone at the outfitters' camp, when I was so tired I could barely lift one foot in front of the other or when I was unable to figure out how to cross the gate to access my truck. But I didn't lie down to die. Why?

I have asked myself the question many times. I really still don't know the answer, other than I didn't want to leave the woman I loved a widow or my beautiful infant daughter fatherless. There were so many things we had yet to do. As I continuously played the song "Baby Shark" over and over, I kept thinking we had many more mountains to climb, fish to catch and outdoor experiences to share and learn from. It is also not in my genes to give up, regardless of how down I get. When I start something, I don't divert attention until I finish it.

Setting small goals can lead to remarkable achievements.

When you face insurmountable adversity, you get what you focus on. Never was the statement truer than when I crawled and stumbled over tough, challenging terrain more than a dozen kilometres from the attack site to my truck. I kept setting short-term goals of reaching different spots, whether finding and climbing to the main trail, reaching where the horse riders camped, the outfitters' tent, and the gate near where my truck was parked.

The main goal was always to reach safety and get help. The cumulative impact of attaining the smaller ones allowed me to achieve the big one.

I knew if I passed out, there would be little left to find once predators had their fill. Leaving the empty juice boxes every kilometre was one way to show searchers how far I had travelled should I not make it out. It also was a way to measure my achievements. It renewed focus, reinvigorated purpose.

Family comes first.

As Joyce says: "My experience has shown that work or other matters are meaningless if your family or loved ones are injured. It really made me realize what is truly important in life. As a result, I am better at pushing back at work when being asked to work more and more hours instead of having a work-life balance."

Don't take relationships for granted.

Life is busy and sometimes you forget about what is genuinely important. Similar to believing that you are fully prepared to confront danger, you can take relationships for granted. They can become ho-hum if you don't work at them and commit to working to sustain them. Sometimes you simply focus on your own wants and joys and forget what is important to other people in your life, especially your significant other.

There is absolutely no doubt that the mauling brought Joyce and I closer together. It rekindled why we were important to each other and what we meant to each other. It made us once again express our feelings, our hopes and desires.

Joyce says it is also important that the partner of someone who endured a traumatic incident take care of themselves, not just the victim: "Looking back, I likely did not need to visit the hospital every single day and I neglected myself a lot. I only took one day off, and I was also taking care of Abby, who was about eight months old. Jeremy was in good hands at the hospital, and he encouraged me to have fun, but I didn't. It wasn't good for me. It is important to love yourself even when a loved one is injured. It was really hard for me to do."

Don't needlessly abandon your passions in life.

It astounds people how quickly I went back to hunting and into the woods, but there were issues and they had to be addressed. We set clear rules, and they have worked. As Joyce says: "Sometimes you have to let things be when a person is ready to heal and move on. I had a bit of trouble with how fast Jeremy was wanting to go back out hunting again. We went back to counselling for just a bit. I guess it's important to respect a person's own healing process and to seek help if you are having trouble with it."

For me, a major part of the healing has been returning to pursue my passion for the outdoors. I also do much more with the whole family now that we are four. We love camping, fishing and now gardening. I most certainly am less of a risk taker. It was vitally important that I confronted the past and transitioned carefully to a future that still includes the best of what I am passionate about.

Deadly Grizzly Attacks in Alberta

EVERY YEAR, TENS OF THOUSANDS OF ADVENTUROUS people head into the Eastern Slopes and other remote areas of Alberta and return without so much of a scratch. Others are not so fortunate,

Grizzly bears are a majestic and iconic part of the ecosystem and a sighting (hopefully from the car) is an experience never to be forgotten. Many people have had non-contact encounters with bears, partly because of the movement of people and industrial development into what is historically grizzly country. These trends have driven bears into privately owned land, in part due to easy access to a variety of food sources and animals, such as cattle.

In 2017, there were 47 investigations into grizzly incidents in Bear Management Area 4, one of seven Grizzly

Bear Management Areas in Alberta and the one where Jeremy's attack took place; two years later, there were 81 grizzly incidents in the same area. Thirteen of the 2017 cases involved bears charging livestock or humans. Two were categorized as extreme. One of those was Jeremy's encounter. The other happened in early July, when a person geocaching about 60 kilometres south of Sundre, in the Harold Creek area, was surprised and attacked by a grizzly and suffered minor lacerations to his face, legs and arm. Others have since been attacked fatally.

In May 2021, in a three-week period, family and friends mourned the deaths of two people known, among other attributes, for their love and admiration of both nature and the outdoors. Both were killed by grizzly bears within only a few dozen kilometres of where Jeremy was mauled. Both were not far from their homes when attacked. Their deaths demonstrate that it is a wonder Jeremy survived his attack, and how quickly and unexpectedly an encounter with a grizzly can bring tragedy.

David Lertzman, 59, a well-known, multiple-award-winning University of Calgary professor and outdoor enthusiast, was tragically killed in a bear attack on Tuesday, May 4. He was out for his regular evening run on trails he knew by heart in the Waiparous Creek area, a lightly populated and deeply forested landscape about 70 kilometres from the Lodge at Panther River. An investigation concluded that a grizzly attacked him from behind as he ran, pushing him off a high, steep cliff to his death.

In a Facebook post published on May 6, his wife, Sarah Lertzman, said: "I had searched for him myself for two hours early in the night and walked right past the point of attack and saw no sign of it. I was looking for a man in trouble and not for a scene of something that had happened. I did not know the risk to myself in that moment, and I am truly blessed that nothing happened to me, as the officers reminded me repeatedly later... By three in the morning, we knew he was no longer with us."

As Alberta Fish and Wildlife had done with Jeremy, they took bear hair samples for DNA analysis and set up traps to capture the bear. Officers closed the area due to its proximity to the small village while they attempted to locate and capture the bear. The bear was never captured.

Three weeks after David's death, 69-year-old Barbara Collister was found dead and partially buried on her beloved Water Valley property, an environmentally sensitive 114-acre parcel about 40 kilometres south of the Lodge at Panther River.

Barbara was the first female graduate of the master of business administration at the University of Calgary, in 1979. Before retiring in 2016, she had a long career as a project manager at Alberta Health Services, helping to build the new Children's Hospital in Calgary, among other projects. The veteran hiker was attacked while she walked the property her family had purchased in 1987 with the intention of preserving it as a biodiversity refuge. In 2019, the family had announced the formal conservation of the property.

Within five days, Fish and Wildlife officers had captured two large female grizzlies near the site of the attack. One of the bears was lactating but did not appear to be actively nursing and was not accompanied by cubs. The other bear was older, with extremely worn teeth.

DNA samples from both bears confirmed the older grizzly was responsible for the fatal attack. It was euthanized. The tests also concluded neither bear was involved in the fatal attack on David Lertzman. The second bear was later released in a more remote location.

In her obituary notice, Barb's family thanked Inspector Kyle Juneau of Fish and Wildlife Enforcement Services, and the Alberta Bear Response Team, led by John Clarke and John Elias, "for their professional and empathetic help and support."

These two tragedies, both of which happened close to where Jeremy was attacked, stand as a sobering reminder of how blessed he is to be alive today.